INTERNATIONAL HUMAN RIGHTS LAW

INTERNATIONAL HUMAN RIGHTS LAW

RETURNING TO UNIVERSAL PRINCIPLES

Mark Gibney

ROWMAN & LITTLEFIELD PUBLISHERS, INC.
Lanham • Boulder • New York • Toronto • Plymouth, UK

ROWMAN & LITTLEFIELD PUBLISHERS, INC.

Published in the United States of America
by Rowman & Littlefield Publishers, Inc.
A wholly owned subsidary of The Rowman & Littlefield Publishing Group,
Inc.
4501 Forbes Boulevard, Suite 200, Lanham, Maryland 20706
www.rowmanlittlefield.com

Estover Road, Plymouth PL6 7PY, United Kingdom

British Library Cataloguing in Publication Information Available

Library of Congress Cataloging-in-Publication Data

Gibney, Mark.
    International human rights law : returning to universal principles / Mark
Gibney.
        p. cm.
    Includes bibliographical references and index.
    ISBN-13: 978-0-7425-5629-4 (cloth : alk. paper)
    ISBN-10: 0-7425-5629-8 (cloth : alk. paper)
    ISBN-13: 978-0-7425-5630-0 (pbk. : alk. paper)
    ISBN-10: 0-7425-5630-1 (pbk. : alk. paper)
    1. Human rights. I. Title.
    K3240.G53 2008
    341.4'8--dc22
                                    2007037634

Printed in the United States of America

♾™ The paper used in this publication meets the minimum requirements of
American National Standard for Information Sciences—Permanence of Paper
for Printed Library Materials, ANSI/NISO Z39.48-1992.

To my mother

CONTENTS

PREFACE: THE NIGHTMARE   ix

1 INTRODUCTION   1

2 STEP ONE: RESPONSIBILITY   21

3 STEP TWO: TERRITORY   57

4 STEP THREE: ACCOUNTABILITY   85

5 STEP FOUR: REMEDY   115

CONCLUSION   143

INDEX   145

ABOUT THE AUTHOR   149

PREFACE:
THE NIGHTMARE

Darwin's Nightmare is an Oscar-nominated documentary that examines life and death issues in Tanzania. The film's story line can be summarized as follows. European concerns remove tons of Nile Perch from Lake Victoria each day and ship this fish to restaurants and shops back home. This goes on at the same time that there is a massive famine in Tanzania—although no one in the movie seems to make any connection between these two things. However, it is unclear how long these trading practices will continue because the Nile Perch are so aggressive they are eating every other kind of fish, which is having the effect of killing the lake itself. Finally, toward the end of the movie the viewer learns that the airplanes flying to Tanzania from Europe are not arriving empty after all but are bringing massive amounts of small arms that are being used to fight the various civil wars in this area of Africa.

As one might imagine, *Darwin's Nightmare* is a stunning and distressing movie. It is stunning and distressing for its scenes of children sniffing glue and sleeping on the streets, attempting to unconsciously live through horrors that could not be imagined by many of us living on this side of the world. But the movie is stunning and distressing in that it clearly shows a connection between the West and people who we previously had thought existed a world apart from us.

But what should be even more stunning and distressing is that it is by no means clear that anyone has done anything wrong or illegal, or at least wrong or illegal under present international law. Take the shipping of arms to Africa. Of all the things that Africans need—food, schools, medicine, clothing, roads, building materials, and so on—the very *last* thing would be weapons, which will only serve to fuel the incredible levels of violence that already exist there. The sending states—and here it has to be said that the five permanent members of the Security Council are among the largest exporters of military weapons—most certainly know this (Yanik 2006).

But what Western states also know is that under international law there is nothing wrong or illegal about selling weapons to another state, even if the sending state is fully aware that these weapons will be used to target civilians or used to commit widespread human rights violations. In the parlance of international law, this is known as the law on state responsibility. However, as I will explain in more detail, what we are really speaking about is the law on state (non)responsibility.

The same can be said for taking food away from Tanzanians, or at least most of the food. In that regard, some of the most wrenching scenes from *Darwin's Nightmare* are those showing local people trying to scavenge something—anything—from the fish skeletons that are thrown away and left behind. According to the International Covenant on Economic, Social and Cultural Rights, one leg of the so-called International Bill of Rights, states obligate themselves to "take steps, individually and through international assistance and cooperation," to achieve "progressively the full realization of the rights recognized in the present Covenant." However, the only "international assistance and cooperation" evident in the film is that which *deprives* Tanzanians of their human rights, rather than that which *protects* human rights.

The lament of those who watch *Darwin's Nightmare* will be that something has to be done about this. Invariably, this "something" will be a call for our compassion and our money. These things are fine, but they do not take us anywhere near as far as we have to go. Money is always in short supply, and our compassion has a funny way of eventually deserting other people. What must be done instead is to change our understanding of human rights.

International Human Rights Law situates itself at the juncture between the great promise of human rights and a reality where hundreds of millions (if not billions) of people in the world are without human rights protection. The overarching theme of the book is that the primary reason for this criminal state of affairs is that there has been a systematic and fundamental misreading of international human rights law itself. Notwithstanding near-universal declarations of the universality of human rights, there has been almost nothing that is "universal" or even "international" about international human rights law. Rather, states have (universally) come to interpret international human rights law in purely domestic terms, seeing their human rights obligations as beginning—but, more importantly, as ending—at their own territorial borders, and they have been given license to interpret international law in this way by some of the leading judicial bodies in the world, most notably the International Court of Justice, the European Court of Human Rights, and the U.S. Supreme Court.

This book is fueled by a general disgust with the failure of human rights law but also by the hope that international human rights law might actually achieve what it was supposed to do in the first place, namely, protect human beings.

REFERENCE

Yanik, Lena K. 2006. "Guns and Human Rights: Major Powers, Global Arms Transfers, and Human Rights Violations." *Human Rights Quarterly* 28:357–88.

1

INTRODUCTION

Although this might be difficult to fathom, until a relatively short time ago the manner in which a state treated its own citizens—no matter how savagely it behaved or the levels of political violence and terror it carried out—was not considered to be a proper "concern" of any other country. Rather, this issue was treated as a purely "domestic" matter, beyond the purview of the international community and international law itself. Or, to use an example from this period, if Nazi Germany had not invaded other countries but had simply sought to eliminate the entire Jewish population within its own territorial borders, this would not have constituted a violation of international law, as incredible as this now seems.

Thus, one of the great advances of the human rights revolution—the international human rights law and institutions that came into existence following World War II—was to eliminate this enormous blind spot. And at the present time, how a state treats its own citizens is most certainly a concern of the entire international community—at least in theory. In this way, countries that abuse their own citizens and violate their human rights are no longer allowed to hide behind the principle of state sovereignty as they had been able to do in the past.

Where international human rights law has largely failed, however, is in coming to terms with the fact that human rights violations occur not only at the hands of one's own government but also through the actions (or inactions) of other states, as well as institutions such as transnational corporations and even international organizations. Consider, then, a hypothetical situation also from the Nazi era. Say that, before the United States entered the war against Germany and Japan in December 1941, the American government had been selling gas ovens to Germany, with full and complete knowledge that these ovens were being used to kill Jews. One would think, quite naturally, that in doing so the U.S. government would be violating international law. After all, the United States would be supplying the Nazis with the very means of extermination. This, however, would not be correct. Yet, what is perhaps even more incredible is that such actions would almost certainly not constitute a violation of international law even today.

For centuries, the notion of "state sovereignty" was used as a shield by oppressive governments. Fortunately, since the end of World War II we are well past this kind of thinking and states are no longer able to hide behind this principle—at least as it relates to their own domestic populations. However, the notion of sovereignty still serves to protect against other forms of state responsibility, only now it is far more likely that countries will be able to hide behind the sovereignty of another state in order to remove themselves from any and all responsibility in assisting an outlaw state. Because of this, while international law is (now) capable of understanding "wrongs" committed by a state against its own population, it remains almost completely incapable of addressing "wrongs" that a state has carried out against people in foreign lands. Essentially what we explore here are all these "other" wrongs—especially those carried out by Western states.

This book, then, provides a vastly different vision of human rights than is currently in use, both in terms of the *responsibility* for violating human rights and in terms of the *protection* of human rights. Human rights has evolved into something that it was never intended to become. Rather than being based firmly on universal principles and values, "human rights" has instead become parochial, territorial, and ultimately self-serving. Much worse, and in large part as a result of this approach, "human rights" has offered almost none of the protection that it promises or that its framers intended.

What is called for here is a return to core, universal principles. What universality means, quite simply, is that, while states are responsible for the human rights violations they carry out within their own domestic borders, they can also be responsible for violating human rights outside their own borders (in places like Guantanamo Bay, Cuba, for example).

Furthermore, while international human rights law creates certain domestic human rights obligations, this same law also creates international or extraterritorial obligations that countries are also bound by. This return to universal principles should not be read to mean that all states (particularly Western states) are responsible for all things for all people. But what also has to be rejected is the dominant thinking that a state has absolutely no human rights obligations outside of its own borders. Thus, what is needed is a completely new way of thinking about these issues concerning the extent of a state's human rights obligations, and it is hoped that this book serves this purpose.

WHAT ARE HUMAN RIGHTS?

Human rights are a core set of rights that human beings possess by simple virtue of their humanity. These rights are best spelled out in a number of international human rights instruments, most notably, the so-called International Bill of Rights consisting of the Universal Declaration of Human Rights (UDHR), the International Covenant on Economic, Social and Cultural Rights (Economic Covenant), and the International Covenant on Civil and Political Rights (Political Covenant). Without attempting to provide an exhaustive list, human rights include the following:

- the right to life, liberty, and security of the person (UDHR, Art. 3)
- the right to be free from torture or to cruel, inhuman, or degrading treatment or punishment (UDHR, Art. 5)
- the right to an effective remedy by the competent national tribunals for violations of human rights (UDHR, Art. 8)
- the right to work (UDHR, Art. 23)
- the right to education (UDHR, Art. 26)
- the right to social security (UDHR, Art. 22)

Human rights are universal—that is, every person has human rights. What does not matter is a person's nationality, where a person resides, how much money a person has (or does not have), or even whether one's government has become a state party to any particular human rights treaty or not. In that way, although the United States is not a party to the International Convention on the Rights of the Child—in fact, it is one of only two countries in the world (Somalia is the other one) that has not signed and ratified this treaty—this does not mean that American children do not have human rights. Rather, all that this means is that the U.S. government has decided (as it has every right to decide) that it will protect the human rights of American children by domestic, rather than by international, means.

Human rights are not complicated, nor should they be made to be complicated. Human rights are sometimes derided for being a utopian wish list of human desires; however, the exact opposite is true. Human rights are not about luxuries, and they are certainly not about mere desires either. Rather, human rights are better thought of as the basic minimum that each individual has to have in order to live a human (rather than an inhuman) existence. Even with these modest and achievable aims, and despite the repeated promise in every single international human rights treaty that human rights are to be enjoyed by "everyone" and denied to "no one," vast numbers of people are left without human rights protection. In terms of economic rights alone, Thomas Pogge has compiled this partial list of human rights violations:

> Out of a total of 6.2 billion human beings (2002), some 799 million are malnourished, more than 880 million lack access to basic health services, 1 billion are without adequate shelter, 1.1 billion without access to safe drinking water, 2 billion without electricity, and 2.4 billion without access to basic sanitation. In addition, 876 million adults are illiterate and over 200 million children between 5 and 14 do wage work outside their household, often under harsh or cruel conditions. Some 50,000 human deaths per day, fully a third of all human deaths, are due to poverty-related causes, and therefore avoidable insofar as poverty itself is avoidable. (Pogge 2005: 3–4)

THE OBLIGATION TO PROTECT HUMAN RIGHTS

Who is responsible for this colossal failure? Without question, the primary responsibility for protecting human rights lies with those states where these individuals who are being denied human rights protection live. Thus, if there are children in Uganda who are not receiving an education, this represents a human rights violation on the part of the

Ugandan government because this state has the primary responsibility for protecting this right (and all other human rights) for all those who reside in Uganda (whether they are Ugandan citizens or not). Unfortunately, this is as far as our thinking has gone—and "primary" responsibility has come to be interpreted as "sole" responsibility. This view is not only seriously deficient in ethical terms, but it also represents a perversion of international human rights law itself.

In my view, the single best treatment on the nature and extent of human rights obligations is Henry Shue's short (but elegant) article "Mediating Duties" (Shue 1988). Shue's analysis differs from my own approach in two significant ways, although we end up arriving at much the same place. The first is that Shue is speaking of moral obligations while my ultimate concern is with legal obligations. The second difference is that Shue's primary focus is individual responsibility, while my concern is with the obligations of states. Still, Shue tends to blend these two together by devoting much of his analysis to the need for establishing an institutional framework in order to carry out the obligations that individuals possess. As I will spend much of the book explaining, I believe this framework already exists in the form of international human rights law.

Moral Obligations

To purposely simplify his approach, Shue divides obligations into two basic categories: negative and positive. If an obligation is negative it requires us not to do things, but if it is positive it requires us to do things. Although these might seem to be mutually exclusive categories, they are not. Rather, there will oftentimes be gradations between what is a "negative" obligation or a "positive" obligation. Consider the scenario depicted in the documentary *Darwin's Nightmare* where European concerns (businesses and states alike) are engaged in shipping tons of Nile Perch fish each day to Europe in the midst of a famine in Tanzania. If European states were to respond to the famine by providing food assistance, this would be a clear case of a positive obligation. If, on the other hand, the European response was simply to halt any further shipment of fish from Tanzania during the famine (which, by the way, was not done), it is not clear how this would be categorized. To some extent this could be viewed as a positive obligation because the European parties concerned would be doing something—they would be halting their trading practices, which they might have a "right" to do (at least in one sense) according to some trade agreement. On the other hand, not removing fish seems to be considerably different than actually providing food. In that way, this begins to look more like a negative obligation. The larger point is that the differences between these two categories might not be as separate and distinct as they might first appear.

The more pertinent question is how far each of these obligations extends. Shue posits that negative obligations are universal, meaning that every person has an obligation to the rest of mankind not to cause harm. What does not matter, or at least what should not matter, is who these people are and where they live. Thus, negative obligations cover all grounds: they are territorial and extraterritorial alike. Yet, despite their universal nature, negative obligations should not prove to be a terrible burden to meet, or as Shue puts it, "I can easily leave alone at least five billion people, and as many more as you like." (Shue 1978:690)

One problem, of course, is what it means to leave people "alone." In that way, it could be that we might actually be causing harm to other people (or are a part of an enterprise that is doing so) and yet not have the slightest inkling of this. Certainly, when a European resident purchases Nile Perch in his local grocery store, there is no intent to worsen famine conditions in Tanzania. In fact, it is very unlikely that the consumer would even know where the fish came from, never mind the social and economic conditions that exist in that particular country. On the other hand, it is almost certain that his government knows a lot more—and perhaps even played a central role in establishing these trading practices in the first place.

Setting these issues aside, the notion of negative obligations should be a fairly easy and uncontroversial concept to understand and to accept. Most, if not all, would agree that it is wrong to harm other people—whether it is our neighbors, our compatriots, or even people in faraway lands. Yet, as we will see in several of the chapters that follow, states have found a number of ways of minimizing or even ignoring their negative obligations.

Positive obligations are seemingly more problematic but for different reasons. For one thing, positive obligations do not have the same intuitive grounding that negative obligations do. Positive obligations entail giving up something that someone has, and people (as well as states) seem loath to do this—even if this "something" is something that the person has no valid claim to possess. What also seems troubling is the fear that there will be no limiting principle. As pointed out earlier, there are literally hundreds of millions of people in the world whose subsistence rights are not being met. The problem is that this "nightmare" has prompted much more fear than action—fear that Western people will be forced to severely change their lives. This, however, grossly overstates the extent of our positive obligations. Unlike negative obligations, positive obligations are not universal, and there are decided constraints on the extent of our positive obligations. Shue explains,

> Universal rights . . . entail not universal duties but full coverage. Full coverage can be provided by a division of labor among duty bearers. All negative duties fall upon everyone, but the positive duties need to be divided up and assigned among bearers in some reasonable way. Further, a reasonable assignment of duties will have to take into account that the duties of any one individual must be limited, ultimately because her total resources are limited and, before that limit is reached, because she has her own rights, which involve the perfectly proper expenditures on some resources on herself rather than fulfilling duties toward others. . . . One cannot have substantial positive duties toward everyone, even if everyone has basic rights. The positive duties of any one individual must be limited. (Shue 1988: 690–91)

No individual has the responsibility to save the world and no state does either. However, what is demanded is "full coverage." This point is a simple one but a vital one. You cannot proclaim human rights as being "universal" but then ignore the fact that enormous numbers of people are left without human rights protection. What is needed is a system of human rights protection. The human rights "system" that presently exists is really no system at all, best evidenced by the fact that, on average, 50,000 people die every single day of preventable causes.

Although there is much to commend Shue's approach, where I think his analysis is much weaker is in his classification of categories of those we are responsible to. Shue rejects the concentric-circle model of moral responsibilities and instead adopts a dual-level approach: one for family, friends, and intimates, and then a different set of obligations for all those he terms "strangers." He writes,

What is wrong with the concentric-circle image of duty is not that it has a center that is highlighted. What is wrong is the progressive character of the decline in priority as one reaches circles farther from the center. What is wrong is the evident assumption that, for example, positive duties to the people who are represented by the fourth ripple out are only half as strong as duties to people represented by the second ripple, and that, in general, positive duties to distant strangers decline, for all practical purposes, to nothing, given limited resources. (Shue 1988: 692)

He continues,

I can imagine strong reasons for priority to intimates—priority to people at the center. Once the center has been left behind, however, I see insufficient reason to believe that one's positive duties to people in the next county, who are in fact strangers, are any greater than one's positive duties to people on the next continent, who, though they are distant strangers, are not any more strangers than the strangers in the next county: a stranger is a stranger. (Shue 1988: 692–93)

I find this thinking rather, well, strange. Certainly there are people living in the next county (or on our own street, for that matter) whom we do not know any better than a person who lives on a different continent. However, this does not necessarily make our county cousins "strangers" to us. These are, after all, people with whom we share the same national government and people with whom we share the same system of national defense. We might even share some of the same schools, roads, and storm sewer systems with these "strangers." More importantly, our (shared) national government bears the primary responsibility for protecting our human rights. This simply is not true of individuals living on another continent.

On the other hand, I believe that Shue is absolutely correct in his thinking that we have failed to extend the scope of our moral obligations, not only to those a continent away, but even in those instances where we might share a national border (as in the case of the United States and Mexico). Shue's explanation is that responsibility follows causality, and because it used to be virtually impossible to affect the lives of people in other countries without actually going there, outsiders naturally have concluded that their moral sphere did not extend to areas of the globe where their influence (both positive and negative) could not be felt. What has changed markedly, of course, is this ability to affect change even in the most remote parts of the world. Shue uses this example to highlight the inter-connectedness among all people: "A vote in Washington to change the wheat price supports in Nebraska can change the price of bread in Calcutta and the price of meat in Kiev." (Shue 1988:694) If morality follows causality, as Shue suggests it does, it will simply be a matter of time before the scope of our moral thinking comes to reflect our expanded global influence.

I do not find this argument persuasive. Rather, I believe that there is a more fundamental explanation for our moral parochialism, namely, this is how morality is taught—in the United States, for sure, but to a large extent in every other country as well. In that way, I agree with Thomas Pogge who argues that the reason massive levels of world poverty continue to exist is simply because this is not viewed as a moral issue, at least not in Western states.

> Extensive severe poverty can continue, because we do not find its eradication morally compelling. And we cannot find its eradication morally compelling until we find its persistence and the relentless rise in global inequality troubling enough to warrant serious moral reflection. (Pogge 2002: 3)

Perhaps Shue is correct and at some point a cosmopolitan ethics will begin to emerge. This certainly is to be encouraged and worked for. But rather than waiting for this day to arrive, I am of the mind that our time and attention would be better spent attending to the legal obligations that we possess already. We now turn to these.

Legal Obligations

There is a common misperception that human rights are simply moral rights—but nothing else. Certainly, there is a moral component for why we protect human rights, but there is a legal component as well. We protect human rights not only because it is the "right" thing to do but also because it is something that the law—our own law—compels us to do. In that way, one of the greatest accomplishments over the past half century or more is the establishment of international human rights law. Under this law, states have willingly, knowingly, and purposely agreed to be bound by the provisions in various human rights treaties—that is, they have signed and ratified certain international treaties (but perhaps declined to join others) and thereby have made this particular aspect of international law a part of their own domestic law. Thus, it is a false notion that there is a separation between international law and domestic law because states that are party to an international human rights treaty are themselves removing any significant distinction between these two.

Ironically enough, the problem that has emerged is not that international human rights law is too "international" but, rather, that it is too "domestic." Or as I stated earlier, there is almost nothing that is "international" about international human rights law. Unfortunately and inexplicably enough, states have come to see human rights in purely domestic terms—but almost nothing beyond that.

One of the overriding goals of this book, then, is to show how international human rights law should properly be read. It is well and good that states have come to recognize (in theory at least) the domestic obligations that arise under international human rights law. However, what has been quite unfortunate is that states have failed to grasp the idea that an international human rights treaty is, after all, an international treaty—with specific international (or what I will more commonly refer to as extraterritorial) obligations. To be clear, this is not meant to suggest that states have the same human rights obligations outside their territorial borders as they do domestically because this is simply not the case. As I have already said before (and as I will repeat perhaps too many times) there is no question that the primary duty to protect human rights rests with the territorial state. There are two reasons for this. The first involves principles of international law. It is always lawful for a state to operate within its own territorial borders but seldom (if ever) lawful for one state to operate within the territorial jurisdiction of another state. The second reason is efficiency. As a general rule, it would not make much sense for State A to be responsible for human rights protection in State B, especially if State B is some distance away.

Although each state has primary responsibility for protecting human rights within its own borders, there are two mistakes that are commonly made concerning human rights, and both of these are central to the present discussion. The first mistake is the commonly accepted idea that human rights protection is based on citizenship. Because we live in a world of nation-states, perhaps it should not be totally surprising that the notion of human rights has come to be subsumed into the broader social contract between rulers and citizens within each society. The problem, however, is that human rights are not based on contractarian or communitarian values but on universal values. Thus, when Ghana offers human rights protection, it does so (or should do so) based on a person's humanity—and not because the recipients of this protection happen to be Ghanaian citizens or not.

The second mistake relates to the extent of a state's human rights obligations. All states—or at least all Western states—act as if their human rights obligations end (rather suddenly, arbitrarily, and conveniently, I might add) at their own territorial boundaries. This is not only a misreading of a number of provisions in various treaties that explicitly demand an extraterritorial application, but it also represents a fundamental misunderstanding of international human rights law itself. The point is this. The entire premise behind all international human rights instruments is that Swedes are not only concerned with the well-being of other Swedes, and Nigerians are not solely concerned with the well-being of other Nigerians, and so on. Rather, in becoming a party to an international human rights treaty, the Nigerian government and the Nigerian people are proclaiming (legally and otherwise) that they are also concerned with the well-being of Swedes, as well as nationals of all other countries. It is tempting to say that it is simply not possible to interpret international human rights law in any other way, yet we know from decades of experience that just the opposite has been true. If human rights protection were something that individual states could (and would) do individually, there would be no need for any international conventions.

A HUMAN RIGHTS HYPOTHETICAL

By way of introducing many of the issues that will be addressed in this book, consider a hypothetical that has a number of real world aspects to it. Assume that all of the countries in the hypothetical are members of most of the major international human rights treaties, including the Torture Convention.

> State A systematically tortures those who are thought to be opponents or critics of the government.

State B does not carry out torture itself. However, it sends torture equipment to State A.

State C does not carry out torture itself. However, it trains agents of State A in the "art" of torture.

State D does not carry out torture itself. However, it allows agents of State A to torture citizens of State A within its territorial borders.

State E does not torture its own citizens. However, its agents torture citizens of State A—at the behest and under the direction of State A.

State F does not carry out torture itself. However, it allows security agents of State A who have allegedly carried out torture to remain free within State F's borders.

State G does not carry out torture itself. However, it has instituted visa requirements for citizens of State A, which has had the effect of severely reducing the number of citizens of State A who are able to flee that country and apply for asylum in State G.

State H does not carry out torture itself, and it does not have a visa requirement for citizens of State A. However, State H has denied nearly all asylum claims filed by citizens of State A, including those alleging past torture, and it has returned nearly all of these individuals to State A.

State I does not carry out torture itself, and it has granted refugee status to large numbers of torture victims of State A. These victims have attempted to have State I bring an inter-state complaint against State A under the Torture Convention. However, the government of State I refuses to do so.

State J does not carry out torture itself, and it has granted refugee status to large numbers of torture victims of State A. However, when these refugees have sought to bring a lawsuit against State A in J's domestic courts for the atrocities carried out against them by agents of State A, these cases have been dismissed on the basis of State J's law that provides sovereign immunity to foreign states—even those accused of committing human rights violations.

State K does not carry out torture itself. However, one of its citizens has been tortured while visiting State A. Upon his return to State K, this individual files a suit against State A. However, the case is dismissed on the grounds of sovereign immunity.

To start off with basics, there is no question that State A violates international human rights law. This is an "easy" case, and for the most part such questions will not be of any concern to us. It remains a fact of life that there are still a lot of bad people and bad governments in the world that do a lot of bad things. Nothing that is said in this book should be interpreted as rationalizing or protecting the behavior of the likes of State A.

The problem is that we never get beyond any of this. Rather, the dominant approach is for states to shake their collective finger at State A—and, unfortunately, that is the end of matters. However, I believe that the more vexing, the more interesting, but also the more important questions relate to the behavior of all of the other countries in this hypothetical. More than that, I am also convinced that human rights protection could improve dramatically—and virtually overnight—if these other countries did not engage in the kinds of activities and practices that they do. In short, to what extent are States B through K also violating human rights? This, essentially, is our inquiry.

FOUR (EASY) STEPS?

The approach I take is to present four steps, or measures, that would greatly improve the protection of human rights in the world. I refer to these steps as "easy" for several reasons. One is that many of the things that I call for exist already in international law. Thus, in a number of instances it is only a matter of recognizing and honoring the obligations that states already possess. On the other hand, there are times when I call for a different interpretation or an expansion of present law. However, I think the reader will find these re-workings consistent with the object and purpose of the human rights treaty in question. Moreover, although I do not spend any time on this issue, many of the changes that I propose (such as changes in the law on state responsibility) are very much in line with domestic practices. Finally, let me point out that perhaps the most far-ranging proposal that I make here—using domestic courts in foreign lands to enforce human rights—already has some legal precedent. In fact, one of the cases (*Al-Adsani v. United Kingdom*) that I analyze under the fourth step (Remedy) was decided by the slenderest (9-8) of margins.

Step One: Responsibility

Whether we are willing to acknowledge it or not, the Western conception of human rights is really about the practices of other states—but never our own. One reason Western people have adopted this worldview is that it tends to make us look good. But another possible reason might be that our "wrongs" might not be "international wrongs" after all.

When I wrote earlier in the context of *Darwin's Nightmare* that there was apparently nothing illegal about shipping military weapons to another state even when there was full knowledge that these arms would be used to carry out gross and systematic human rights abuses, I was referencing the International Court of Justice ruling in *Nicaragua v. United States* (1986), which set forth an impossibly high standard for establishing state responsibility in situations of "aiding and abetting" human rights violations. What the *Nicaragua* standard does is to allow states to arm and equip and be aligned with states that carry out massive levels of human rights violations, and yet the state that provides this material support will bear *none* of the responsibility for any of these abuses—unless it had exercised nearly absolute control over the actions of the receiving state (or some other entity). What this means in the real world is that international law allows states to get away with murder—so long as the sending state has not actually pulled the trigger, so to speak.

The first step, then, is to recognize how completely deficient the law on state responsibility is and to re-interpret and/or re-configure this law so that it captures much more fully the extent to which "other" states might be complicit in the violation of human rights. An easy case, I would think, would be arming and equipping a murderous dictatorship. To me, this behavior literally "shocks the conscience." But what is even more shocking is the fact that international law gives states license to do exactly that. However, there are other kinds of actions that states take that are not nearly as visible as this but that also have devastating consequences in terms of human rights protection in other lands. What I propose is a very basic standard but one that differs considerably from the various tests in international law that presently exist: to what extent is a state instrumental in helping to bring about violations of human rights?

Step Two: Territory

Western states have come to adopt some rather bizarre ideas concerning where their own human rights obligations begin and end. The dominant, if not universal, view is that a state is able to do things outside its territory that it is prohibited from doing within its own domestic borders. States, of course, do not publicly proclaim this position. However, this is implicit in the positions they collectively maintain. I focus on several judicial decisions to explore this point. The first is the U.S. Supreme Court decision in *Sale v. Haitians Centers Council* (1993), which challenged the U.S. Coast Guard's interdiction program on the grounds that the United States was sending Haitian boatpeople back to their country where they would face the likelihood of danger, in violation of both domestic (U.S.) and international human rights law. The Supreme Court rejected this argument and upheld the interdiction program on the grounds that the U.S. government's obligation not to send a person back to a country where she or he would face the likelihood of harm (what in international law is termed nonrefoulement) did not arise unless and until a person had reached American soil—but not on the high seas.

The second case we examine is the European Court of Human Rights (ECHR) decision in *Bankovic et al. v. Belgium et al.* (2001). This case was based on a North Atlantic Treaty Organisation (NATO) bombing mission over Belgrade in 1999 that killed and/or injured a group of civilians. The question presented was whether citizens of a country (Yugoslavia) that is not a party to the European Convention on Human Rights could receive any protection under it. The Court rejected this position in this case, holding that the European Convention is "essentially" or "primarily" territorial, and that only under "exceptional circumstances" can individuals outside of Europe receive Convention protection. Furthermore, not only are European states not bound by the Convention when they operate outside of "Europe" (absent the existence of "exceptional circumstances," which are deemed as such after the fact), but apparently these states are not bound by almost any other international human rights treaty either, at least according to the Court's view that most other international human rights instruments are also without extraterritorial effect.

The third example involves the "war on terror." The entire premise behind the Bush administration's policy of holding "enemy combatants" in foreign military bases such as Guantanamo Bay, Cuba, was so that neither U.S. domestic law nor American obligations under international law would be applicable. Thus, the entire point of using offshore detention facilities was to create a legal "black hole" (there is no other word for it) where no legal obstacles (or protections) were thought to apply. To some extent, the U.S. Supreme Court has rejected this reasoning. However, territory still plays an enormously important role in all this, although it is not exactly clear how and why this should be.

What each of these examples shows is that Western states work under the assumption that international human rights law allows them to operate one way at home—but in a completely different manner outside their territorial borders. One thing that makes this approach to human rights protection so difficult to understand is that in each of these cases what we are talking about are negative obligations—the duty not to cause harm. As noted in our discussion of Shue, negative obligations are universal, meaning that we are not to harm anyone else. In addition, negative obligations would seem to be far less controversial than positive obligations would be. Yet, if states are not even willing to recognize their negative obligations to those outside their own borders, is there any prospect that they will honor their positive obligations?

Step Three: Accountability

Contrary to the dominant thinking, international human rights law is replete with positive extraterritorial obligations. One of the clearest examples of this is to be found in Article 2 (1) of the Economic Covenant:

> Each State Party to the present Covenant undertakes to take steps, individually and *through international assistance and cooperation*, especially economic and technical, to the maximum of its available resources, with a view to achieving progressively the full realization of the rights recognized in the present Covenant by all appropriate means, including particularly the adoption of legislative measures (emphasis supplied).

The third step is quite straightforward: states should be held accountable for the human rights obligations that they have agreed to be bound by. Countries are not required to become a party to any international human rights conventions—that is, there is no entity that is holding a gun to its head forcing a country to become a state party to the Torture Convention or the Economic Covenant or the Political Covenant or the Convention on the Rights of the Child, and so on. However, when countries do become state parties they thereby undertake certain legal obligations. Some of these obligations are domestic;

other obligations extend beyond the domestic setting. The language emphasized above is an example of an extraterritorial obligation. The point is that states must carry out all of the obligations they have agreed to be bound by—and they should be held accountable when they fail to do so.

Step Four: Remedy

Undoubtedly, the gravest failure of all is that while international human rights law has done a superb job of imbuing individuals with an impressive set of rights, it has done an abysmal job of providing individuals with the means of enforcing these rights. If international human rights law is intended to be nothing more than a theoretical construct with no practical application, then this fact needs to be acknowledged immediately. If, however, international human rights law is actually intended to do what it was intended to do and what it promises to do, then it must do a vastly better job of enforcing the law that exists.

The problem with the present system of human rights enforcement is that it actually works to disempower human beings as opposed to empowering individuals as it was intended to do. In that way, human rights victims are doubly victimized. They are victimized when the human rights violation first occurs. But they are victimized a second time when they are denied the "effective remedy" that international human rights law promises to provide them. The point is that both of these are violations of international law.

I do not have any faith in the present system for the simple reason that it is in large part based on the premise that the state that is responsible for violating human rights will (somehow) then turn around and enforce the law—against itself. Several decades of massive levels of human rights violations have proven just the opposite to be true. Yet, international human rights law has shown absolutely no inclination to do anything to change this "system."

But states that carry out human rights violations directly are not the only ones that should be faulted. Rather, the rest of the world community has also played an essential role in helping to perpetuate this state of affairs. Thus, while states that engage in torture (to focus on one atrocity) have seldom (if ever) provided an effective remedy for those it has victimized, the record of "outside" states has been equally ineffective—and in many ways just as offensive to the idea of protecting human rights. This is not to say that certain victories have not been achieved. The international effort to extradite and prosecute General Pinochet, the former Chilean dictator, is certainly commendable and to be celebrated. Yet, rather serving as the springboard in terms of bringing tens of thousands of other officials to justice, the *Pinochet* case has had almost the opposite effect.

To repeat my earlier complaint, there has been almost nothing international about international law. Not a single state has ever filed an inter-state complaint against another state under the international system. Not a single state has brought a claim against another state before the International Court of Justice based on the human rights violations of this other state. And not a single state has allowed human rights victims to sue an offending state in its courts. In short, countries that violate human rights (directly) have had an enormous amount of help and support—and in large part this help and support has been from "Us."

Several years ago I made an argument in favor of creating an International Civil Court that would complement the newly created International Criminal Court (Gibney 2002). The Civil Court that I envision would allow victims themselves to bring a legal action against their own state (and other states as well) for violating their human rights. I am still convinced of the merits of this idea, and I spend a small amount of time reiterating these arguments. But I also examine two other proposals.

The first is Manfred Nowak's recent call for the establishment of a World Court of Human Rights within the U.N. system (Nowak 2007). To accomplish this, what would be needed would be a new international treaty—the Statute of the World Court of Human Rights—that would come into existence after a sufficient number of states, as provided in the treaty, had ratified the Statute. According to Nowak's proposal, states would not only be free to choose whether to ratify the Statute or not, but they would also be able to decide what rights they would be subjected to under the Court's jurisdiction.

The other proposal attempts to avoid having to create any new international institutions but to make use of already existing domestic courts—only the domestic courts of states other than where the human rights violations allegedly took place. Under this scheme, and employing the hypothetical used earlier, torture victims from State A would be able to use the domestic courts of each of the other parties to the Torture Convention to pursue an "effective remedy" against State A. Although this proposal will seem quite strange to many, as I noted before, there has been at least some judicial attention to this matter, albeit with disappointing results. The first case is the U.S. Supreme Court's decision in *Saudi Arabia v. Nelson* (1993). The case centered on the claim of an American citizen who had been tortured in Saudi Arabia by Saudi agents and who attempted to sue that government in U.S. court. The Court upheld the dismissal of the suit based on its reading of the Foreign Sovereign Immunity Act (FSIA), which grants foreign states immunity in U.S. courts—subject to several exceptions. The most serious deficiency in the Court's approach is that it gives virtually no heed to the entire concept of human rights. Rather, *Nelson* is little more than an exercise in statutory construction of the meaning of the term "commercial activity." What the Court should have done instead is to probe the various inconsistencies between the FSIA and U.S. obligations under international human rights law.

The second case is the European Court of Human Rights decision in *Al-Adsani v. United Kingdom* (2001), which was based on a claim brought by a dual national (British and Kuwait) who claimed to have been tortured in Kuwait during the first Persian Gulf War. Al-Adsani's claim against the United Kingdom was that the dismissal of his suit against the Kuwaiti government by British courts was itself a violation of the European Convention.

One of the great fears driving the Court's decision in *Al-Adsani* was the perceived overload problem. In other words, although the Court seemed more than a bit unsettled with its own ruling—which allowed a state party to the European Convention to grant sovereign immunity protection to a country that has tortured one of its own citizens—one of the rationales that it relied upon was that an opposite holding would create a veritable floodgate of cases in European courts. Thus, the great concern is that if the (European) courtroom door were to be opened just a little, the various judicial systems of these states (not to mention the European Court of Human Rights itself) would quickly come to be inundated with any and all manner of human rights claims.

This thinking, of course, is more than understandable given the levels of human rights violations that exist in the world. Yet, what is never considered is what the world would look like if human rights protection were to be taken seriously—and states that violated human rights were actually held responsible for doing so. What we never stop to consider is that the primary reason human rights are violated with impunity is that states do, in fact, enjoy impunity. This has to stop and this nightmare has to end. This book is intended to show the manner in which this could be accomplished.

REFERENCES

Gibney, Mark. 2002. "On the Need for an International Civil Court." *The Fletcher Forum of World Affairs* 26:47–58.

Nowak, Manfred. 2007. "The Need for a World Court of Human Rights." *Human Rights Law Review* 7:251–59.

Pogge, Thomas. 2002. *World Poverty and Human Rights: Cosmopolitan Responsibilities and Reforms*. Malden, MA: Blackwell Publishing.

——. 2005. "Human Rights and Human Responsibilities," in Andrew Kuper (ed.), *Global Responsibilities: Who Must Deliver on Human Rights?* New York: Routledge.

Shue, Henry. 1988. "Mediating Duties." *Ethics* 98:687–704.

STEP ONE: RESPONSIBILITY

S tate responsibility is concerned with whether a state has committed an "international wrong" or not. In other words, has a state done something (or failed to do something) that puts it in violation of international law? In many instances this will not be a contentious issue. A state that practices torture is "responsible" for doing so; that much is clear. My concern, however, is not so much with "direct" actions such as this but rather with the way in which states pursue policies that have the effect of harming human rights protection in other states, albeit in an indirect manner. The hypothetical posited in the introduction presents a variety of ways in which states either take action—that is, instituting visas, supplying military equipment to a brutal dictatorship—or do not take action—that is, refusing to file an inter-state complaint—that helps lead to the destruction of human rights protection. To what extent are these "other" states also violating international human rights law?

VARIOUS STANDARDS FOR DETERMINING STATE RESPONSIBILITY

International Court of Justice (Part I)

The leading case on this issue is *Nicaragua v. United States*, decided by the International Court of Justice (ICJ) in 1986. By way of brief historical background, the U.S. government opposed the ruling political party (Sandinistas) in Nicaragua on the grounds that they were communists, and it thereby took up measures to remove this group from power. Although American military and security personnel carried out certain direct military actions against the Nicaraguan state such as mining the country's harbors, most American military and political objectives were pursued by aiding and supporting a counter-revolutionary group called the contras.

In response to this, the Nicaraguan government brought a case against the United States before the ICJ based on two grounds. The first was premised on "direct" American action, such as mining Nicaragua's harbors. The second was based on "indirect" actions. In terms of this latter point, in its plea to the ICJ Nicaragua claimed that because of the intimate ties between the United States and the contras, the U.S. government should bear legal responsibility for the human rights violations carried out by this group.

The Court accepted the first argument but rejected the second. The Court held that by training, arming, equipping, financing, and supplying the contra rebel forces, the United States had violated the obligation not to intervene in the affairs of another state. Through its action in armed attacks in Nicaragua, the United States had breached its obligation under customary international law not to use force against another state. And in laying mines in the territorial waters of Nicaragua, the United States was in breach of its obligations not to use force against another country, not to intervene in its affairs, not to violate its sovereignty, and not to interrupt peaceful maritime commerce. In short, the Court found that American agents had engaged in a number of aggressive actions against the Nicaraguan state and because of this the United States had violated international law.

However, it is Nicaragua's other claim that is more pertinent to our present discussion. To what extent is a state responsible for the "aid and assistance" that it provides to those that carry out human rights violations directly? The Court gave considerable attention detailing the long-standing relationship between the contras and the U.S. government, although it rejected Nicaragua's claim that the United States had actually created the contra organization in the first place. Still, the Court concluded that massive levels of American financial and logistical support had in fact fundamentally changed the nature and scope of the contras' operations. Furthermore, the ICJ was quite cognizant of the contras' horrible human rights record.

Yet, despite this, the Court rejected the idea that the United States was responsible for *any* wrongdoing carried out by the contras. In the Court's view, the contras were not totally "dependent" on the United States (at least not for the entire period of time in question) in order to be able to equate the contras with being "an organ of the United States government." The Court explains as follows:

> In sum, the evidence available to the Court indicates that various forms of assistance provided to the contras by the United States have been crucial to the pursuit of their activities, but it is insufficient to demonstrate their complete dependence on the United States aid. On the other hand, it indicates that in the initial years of United States assistance the contra force was so dependent. However, whether the United States Government at any stage devised the strategy and directed the tactics of the contras depends on the extent to which the United States made use of the potential for control inherent in the dependence. The Court already indicated that it has insufficient evidence to reach a finding on this point. (par. 110)

The ICJ returns to this issue at another point in its opinion:

> The Court has taken the view . . . that United States participation, even if preponderant or decisive, in the financing, organizing, training, supplying and equipping of the contras, the selection of its military or paramilitary targets, and the planning of the whole of its operation, is still insufficient in itself, on the basis of the evidence in the possession of the Court, for the purpose of attributing to the United States the acts committed by the contras in the course of their military or paramilitary operations. (par. 115)

The Court proceeds further by announcing what has come to be known as the "effective control" standard:

> All of the forms of United States participation mentioned above, and even the general control by the respondent State over a force with a high degree of dependency on it, would not in themselves mean, without further evidence, that the United States directed or enforced the perpetration of the acts contrary to human rights and humanitarian law alleged by the applicant State. Such acts could well be committed by members of the contras without the control of the United States. For this conduct to give rise to legal responsibility of the United States, it would in principle have to be proved that the State had effective control of the military and

paramilitary operations in the course of which the alleged violations were committed. (par. 115)

What constitutes "effective control"? Perhaps the Court's clearest expression of this standard is as follows: "In light of the evidence and material available to it, the Court is not satisfied that *all* the operations launched by the contra force, at *every* stage of the conflict, reflected strategy and tactics *wholly* devised by the United States" (par. 106, emphases supplied).

There are enormous problems with the *Nicaragua* decision, not only in terms of the standard that it establishes but also in terms of its approach to human rights quite generally (Gibney et al. 1999). The first thing is the level of "control" that the Court demands in order for "state responsibility" to arise in situations involving "aid or assistance." Or to phrase this in a different way, it is next to impossible to conjure up a situation (short of a complete military occupation) where one state would ever be able to exercise this level of control in order to bear responsibility for any of the actions of this other entity. What this means, then, is that a state can be aligned with even the most brutal regimes and provide arms and equipment and logistical support that enable these dictatorships to commit gross and systematic human rights violations—and yet there would be nothing "wrong" or "unlawful" about such policies and actions.

A second problem with the Court's decision is that it treats "state responsibility" as an either-or proposition—that is, either a state exercises the requisite level of "effective control" (as next to impossible as this would be to achieve), in which case the state would be "responsible" for the actions of this other entity—or it does not exercise the required level of "effective control," in which case it will not bear a shred of responsibility. The point is that there is no in-between. There is no attempt to measure various levels of support. There is no attempt to factor in the degree of knowledge that the "sending" state has (or should have) of human rights violations in the "receiving" state or the levels of support that it provides to this state or even the kind of material assistance that is given. Under the *Nicaragua* ruling, quite simply (and simplistically), the United States had not reached this threshold of responsibility, and because it did not it was no more blameworthy than a state that provided absolutely no assistance whatsoever to the contras.

There are several ways that the *Nicaragua* decision might be rationalized. One is to focus on the Court's ruling with respect to the illegality of the "direct" American action in Nicaragua, and thereby focus less on the ICJ's rejection of responsibility based on "indirect" actions (i.e., the support for the contras). Another way to try to rationalize the decision is by acknowledging that the Court took Nicaragua's "indirect" claim seriously, and that it did not summarily dismiss this part of the complaint. In that way, I suppose, states are put on notice that there might be instances where they might be held "responsible" for human rights violations committed by groups and states that they support. Finally, one might try to rationalize away the decision on the basis that the case involved the relationship between a state and a group of non-state actors in another country, with the thinking being that there might be a different (and lower) standard in a situation where there are two states involved—although I would argue that, if anything, this standard would be even higher in this other situation because we would be talking about two sovereign states.

In any event, I am not satisfied with any of these rationales. Setting aside such things as the incredible sloppiness of the decision itself, including the unnecessary confusion engendered by the Court's discussion of "dependence" and the question of how longstanding such dependence would have to be in order for the contras to be "dependent" on the United States, the *Nicaragua* standard is simply anathema to the protection of human rights, and it needs to be recognized as such. The bottom line is that what really prevails is not state responsibility but state (non)responsibility—or worse, the promotion of state irresponsibility. *Nicaragua* says to countries that international law allows them to get in bed, as it were, with the worst of the worst—and yet (somehow) not bear *any* responsibility for *any* of the crimes and human rights violations that might ensue from doing so. In my view, the decision comes straight out of the Dark Ages in terms of its approach to human rights.

International Criminal Tribunal for the Former Yugoslavia

Others have found the *Nicaragua* decision wanting as well. Certainly, the most noteworthy rejection of the "effective control" standard was by the Appeals Court of the International Criminal Court for the Former Yugoslavia (ICTY) in its *Tadic* decision. In this case, the ICTY concluded that the *Nicaragua* standard was not "persuasive," and it arrived at this conclusion based on two grounds. The first is that the *Nicaragua* standard was not consonant with the "very logic of the entire system on State responsibility." The second is that the *Nicaragua* test is "at variance with judicial and state practice."

The ICTY then set forth its own standard (overall control) for determining state responsibility in situations involving "aid and assistance."

> In order to attribute the acts of the military or paramilitary group to a State, it must be proved that the State wields overall control over the group, not only by equipping and financing the group, but also by coordinating or helping in the general planning of its military activity. Only then can the State be held internationally accountable for any misconduct of the group. However, it is not necessary that, in addition, the State should also issue, either to the head or to members of the group, instructions for the commission of specific acts contrary to international law. (par. 131)

After announcing this as its general rule, the ICTY then offered a series of refinements to this standard. One is the distinction between individuals or groups not organized into military structures, on the one hand, and organized militias on the other, the Court being of the view that a higher standard ("specific instructions") was necessary for the former. In terms of the latter,

> by contrast, control by a State over subordinate armed forces or militias or paramilitary units may be of an overall character (and must comprise more than the mere provision of financial assistance or military equipment or training). This requirement, however, does not go so far as to include the issuing of specific orders by the State, or its direction of each individual operation. Under international law it is by no means necessary that the controlling authorities should plan all the operations of the units dependent on them, choose their targets, or give specific instructions concerning the conduct of military operations and any alleged violations of international humanitarian law. (par. 137)

The Court continues,

> The control required by international law may be deemed to exist when a State (or, in the context of an armed conflict, the Party to the conflict) *has a role in organizing, coordinating or planning the military actions* of the

military group, in addition to financing, training and equipping or providing operational support to that group. Acts performed by the group or members thereof may be regarded as acts of *de facto* State organs regardless of any specific instruction by the controlling State concerning the commission of each of those acts. (par. 137, emphasis in original)

And as a final measure, the ICTY added a territorial dimension to its standard, reasoning that there should be a higher degree of control when the sending state is not the territorial state:

Of course, if, as in *Nicaragua*, the controlling State is not the territorial State where the armed clashes occur or where at any rate the armed units perform their acts, more extensive and compelling evidence is required to show that the State is genuinely in control of the units or groups not merely by financing and equipping them, but also by generally directing or helping plan their actions. (par. 138)

To avoid confusion, it cannot be said that the law on state responsibility in situations of "aid and assistance" is settled (Nahapetian 2002). Thus far we have looked at *Nicaragua*'s "effective control" standard and *Tadic*'s "overall control" standard. Between these two, the ICTY's "overall control" standard is superior for the simple reason that it takes a more liberal view of "state responsibility," thereby making more behavior destructive of human rights protection illegal under international law. In other words, the ICTY takes a more realistic approach in that it does not demand that virtually every single action be done under the command of this other entity in order to invoke responsibility.

However, the real question is why "control"—effective, overall, or otherwise—is being used as a legal standard in the first place. The point is that, in their relations with one another, states seldom (if ever) seek to exercise "control" over other entities. This is not to say that states do not attempt to exercise influence over other states and/or to maintain friendly relations as well. States do this (or attempt to do this) all the time. Yet, this is considerably different from the issue of "control," at least as that term is used by either the International Court of Justice or the International Criminal Tribunal for the Former Yugoslavia.

The world's arms trade offers a perfect example of why "control" is simply the wrong standard to apply. Arms sales are used as a way of maintaining friendly relations but also as a way of making money. The point is that when states sell arms they are not trying to exercise the kind of "control" under discussion in either *Nicaragua* or *Tadic*. It strains reality to even think in these terms. But what this also means is that it is lawful for a state to provide whatever weapons it wants, to whatever country or guerrilla group is willing to purchase them—even when the "sending" state might be absolutely certain that these weapons will be used against civilian populations. It is impossible to understand how this "law" can actually be termed the law on state responsibility.

Rather than attempting to gauge the level of "control," a much better approach would be to simply see whether a state's actions are destructive of human rights protection or not. Primary responsibility will always remain with the state that is actually carrying out these atrocities. However, there is no reason why other countries that actively support this outlaw state should not also be held accountable—according to their level of involvement—on the basis of some kind of secondary responsibility.

The questions that would have to be addressed in determining state responsibility under this approach are rather elementary: Does the "receiving" state violate human rights, and does the "sending" state know this (or should it know this)? What kind of material and logistical support does the "sending" state provide, and how is this material being used? It is important to note that this is not an absolute liability standard. For example, if a country sells military hardware to a state with a solid human rights record, but if the receiving state then turns around and uses these weapons against civilian populations, the "sending" state has not done anything that should be considered wrong or unlawful. However, that situation is vastly different from one where a state sells weapons to another state with full knowledge that there is a strong likelihood (and perhaps even near certainty) that these weapons will be used to violate human rights.

International Law Commission

Unfortunately, it is not clear that this is the direction international law is heading in. One of the more recent voices on this issue has come from the International Law Commission (ILC), created by the U.N. General Assembly in 1948 as a step toward fulfilling the United Nations' Charter mandate of "encouraging the progressive development of international law and its codification." In 2001, the ILC completed its decades-long work by submitting its "Draft Articles and State Responsibility" (Crawford 2002). The most pertinent article for our present discussion is Article 16, entitled "Aid or assistance in the commission of an internationally wrongful act," which reads,

> A State which aids or assists another State in the commission of an internationally wrongful act by the latter is internationally responsible for doing so if:
>
> the State does so with knowledge of the circumstances of the internationally wrongful act; and
> the act would be internationally wrongful if committed by that State.

The accompanying Commentary attempts to provide some illumination of the meaning of Article 16. Paragraph 1 of the Commentary reads,

> Article 16 deals with the situation where one State provides aid or assistance to another with a view of facilitating the commission of an internationally wrongful act by the latter. Such situations arise where a State voluntarily assists or aids another State in carrying out conduct which violates the international obligations of the latter, for example, by knowingly providing an essential facility or financing the activity in question. Other examples include providing means for the closing of an international waterway, facilitating the abduction of persons on foreign soil, or assisting in the destruction of property belonging to nationals of a third country. The State primarily responsible in each case is the acting State, and the assisting State has only a supporting role. . . . Under article 16, aid or assistance by the assisting State will only be responsible to the extent that its own conduct has caused or contributed to the internationally wrongful act. Thus, in cases where that internationally wrongful act would clearly have occurred in any event, the responsibility of the assisting State will not extend to compensating for the act itself.

Paragraph 3 of the Commentary then sets forth a standard for determining responsibility:

> Article 16 limits the scope of responsibility for aid or assistance in three ways. First, the relevant State organ or agency providing aid or assistance must be aware of the circumstances making the conduct of the assisted State internationally wrongful; secondly, the aid or assistance must be given with a view to facilitating the commission of that act, and must actually do so; and thirdly, the completed act must be such that it would have been wrongful had it been committed by the assisting State itself.

Paragraph 5 provides further explanation of the second requirement:

> The second requirement is that aid or assistance must be given with a view to facilitating the commission of the wrongful act, and must actually do so. This limits the application of article 16 to those cases where the aid or assistance given is clearly linked to the subsequent wrongful conduct. A State is not responsible for aid or assistance under article 16 unless the relevant organ intended, by the aid or assistance given, to facilitate the occurrence of the wrongful conduct and the internationally wrongful conduct is actually committed by the aided or assisted State. There is no requirement that the aid or assistance should have been essential to the performance of the internationally wrongful act; it is sufficient if it contributed significantly to that act.

Finally, Paragraph 9 underscores that "intent" is the key to finding responsibility:

> The obligation not to provide aid or assistance to facilitate the commission of an internationally wrongful act by another State is not limited to the prohibition on the use of force. For instance, a State may incur responsibility if it assists another State to circumvent sanctions imposed by the United Nations Security Council or provide material aid to a State that uses the aid to commit human rights violations. In this respect, the United Nations General Assembly has called on member States in a number of cases to refrain from supplying arms and other military assistance to countries found to be committing serious human rights violations. Where the allegation is that the assistance of a State has facilitated human rights abuses by another State, the particular circumstances of each case must be carefully examined to determine whether the aiding State by its aid was aware of and intended to facilitate the commission of the internationally wrongful conduct.

Like the *Nicaragua* decision, Article 16 of the International Law Commission's Articles on State Responsibility (which implicitly adopts the *Nicaragua* standard) is destructive of human rights protection, and the reason I say this is that avoiding responsibility under this standard is really quite easy. Countries that ship arms and equipment to states that use this equipment to violate human rights can simply claim that this was not their "intent." Unfortunately, this seems to be the end of the matter.

International Court of Justice (Part II)

The International Court of Justice returned to the issue of state responsibility in 2007 in the *Case Concerning the Application of the Convention on the Prevention of the Punishment of the Crime of Genocide (Bosnia and Herzegovina v. Serbia and Montenegro)*. The ICJ addressed two questions. The first was whether Serbia's close and longstanding relationship with Bosnian Serb forces would thereby make Serbia "responsible" for genocidal acts carried out by the latter. Reaffirming its approach in the *Nicaragua* case, the ICJ applied several extraordinarily stringent standards and it rejected this claim. However, in terms of the second issue— whether the Serbian state had failed to "prevent" and "punish" acts of genocide—the ICJ went in just the opposite direction, applying a rather loose and minimal "influence" standard, and ruling that Serbia had violated these obligations under the Genocide Convention.

One of the problems with *Bosnia v. Serbia* is the Court's halting and timid approach, perhaps best evidenced by its unnecessary treatment of the question whether the Genocide Convention prohibits state parties from carrying out genocide (the answer, of course, is that it does). Related to this, throughout its ruling the ICJ displayed a horrible tendency of treating each and every atrocity as an isolated event—but thereby ignoring larger political trends. This helps to explain the Court's incredulous finding that acts of genocide had only taken place at one time and in one locale: Srebrenica.

This piecemeal approach most certainly affected the ICJ's treatment of the issue of state responsibility. Rather than looking at the totality of Serb actions, including the years that the Serbian state had actively, knowingly, and purposely supported Bosnian Serb paramilitary forces that were carrying out gross and systematic human rights violations (including genocide), the Court seemed content (and intent) in trying to find instances (and they really were only instances) where the aims and goals of the Serbian government and its Bosnian Serbs might not have been exactly the same. This was not especially difficult to find. As I pointed out earlier, there are few (if any) situations where a sending state will be able to direct and control every single action of military or paramilitary forces operating in another land. But this standard leads to absurd and immoral results, as evidenced by the ICJ's ruling in this case that the Serbian government bore no "responsibility" for the acts of genocide carried out by its various Bosnian Serb "allies."

The Court approached this matter by focusing on three separate Articles on State Responsibility. Article 4 is entitled "Conduct of organs of a State," and the question was whether the Bosnian Serbs could be considered "organs" of the Serbian state. The ICJ held that the proper legal standard was whether "complete dependence" could be established, and it concluded (correctly, at least according to this standard) that such a relationship could not be proven in this one case:

> While the political, military and logistical relations between [the Serbian government and the Bosnian Serbs] had been strong and close in previous years . . . and these ties undoubtedly remained powerful, they were, at least at the relevant time, not such that the Bosnian Serbs' political and military organizations should be equated with organs of the FRY. It is even true that differences over strategic options emerged at the time between Yugoslav authorities and Bosnian Serb leaders; at the very least, these are evidence that the latter had some qualified, but real, margin of independence. (par. 394)

The Court then turned to Article 8, entitled "Conduct directed or controlled by a State." Here, the ICJ simply applied the "effective control" test from its *Nicaragua* decision, warning at the outset, "It must . . . be shown that this 'effective control' was exercised, or that the State's instructions were given, in respect of *each* operation in which the alleged violations occurred, not generally in respect of the overall actions taken by the persons or groups of persons having committed the violation" (par. 400, emphasis supplied). Of course, no such level of control could be established.

It was at this juncture that the ICJ took issue with the ICTY's use of the "overall control" standard in *Tadic*, claiming that while such a test would be perfectly appropriate in determining whether a particular conflict was international in scope or not, "overall control" is not the appropriate test in determining "state responsibility." According to the Court, the "overall control" standard "stretches too far, almost to (*sic*) breaking point, the connection which must exist between the conduct of a State's organs and its international responsibility" (par. 406). However, I would suggest that the ICJ has itself taken the principle of state responsibility to its breaking point (and beyond) by refusing to hold states in any way "responsible" for so many of the horrible things they help to do outside their own national borders.

The last Article on State Responsibility that the ICJ examined is Article 16, entitled "Aid or assistance in the commission of an internationally wrongful act," which we spent some time examining earlier. At the outset, the Court pointed out that Article 16 speaks to state-state relations and, thus, was "not directly relevant to the present case" (par. 420). Nonetheless, the ICJ proceeded with its analysis, positing that providing "aid and assistance" to a perpetrator of the crime of genocide "cannot be treated as complicity in genocide unless at the least that organ or person acted knowingly, that is to say, in particular, was aware of the specific intent . . . of the principal perpetrator" (par. 421). According to the Court, this requisite intent could not be proven "beyond any doubt" for the one atrocity (Srebrenica) that it was willing to recognize as genocide.

> A point which is clearly decisive in this connection is that it was not conclusively shown that the decision to eliminate physically the adult male population of the Muslim community from Srebrenica was brought to the attention of the Belgrade authorities when it was taken: the Court has found . . . that that decision was taken shortly before it was carried out, a process which took a very short time (essentially between 13 and 16 July 1995), despite the exceptionally high number of victims. It has therefore not been conclusively established that, at the crucial time, the FRY supplied aid to the perpetrators of the genocide in full awareness that the aid supplied would be used to commit genocide. (par. 423)

In my view, there are several things wrong with the state responsibility aspect of the Court's ruling. One is simply the manner in which the Court reads the record before it, treating each and every atrocity in isolation from those before and those occurring afterwards. The massacre at Srebrenica was certainly a signature event of this brutal conflict, but the Bosnian Serbs' efforts at "ethnic cleansing" were by no means limited to this one atrocity. Beyond this, there is the issue of the Court's insistence on maintaining impossibly high standards for determining state responsibility. It simply did not matter which of the Articles on the Law of State Responsibility that it invoked; in each instance there was the same finding: no responsibility. Furthermore, there is the matter of continuing to treat "responsibility" as an either-or concept, thereby avoiding the issue of degrees of responsibility altogether.

But what makes the Court's approach to the issue of state responsibility even more difficult to understand is the way in which it then treated the issue of whether Serbia had violated its obligations under the Genocide Convention to "prevent" and "punish." Article 1 of the Convention reads, "The Contracting Parties confirm that genocide, whether committed in time of peace or in time of war, is a crime under international law which they undertake to prevent and to punish."

The ICJ began its analysis by noting that the "Genocide Convention is not the only international instrument providing for an obligation on state parties to it to take certain steps to prevent the acts it seeks to prohibit" (par. 429), pointing to the Torture Convention and several other international treaties. The ICJ then ruled that the obligations of state parties were one of conduct and not results. That is, a state is under no obligation to succeed but rather "to employ all means reasonably available to them, so as to prevent genocide as far as possible" (par. 430).

So what are the obligations of state parties? It is here that the Court's ruling becomes far more noteworthy and deserving of being quoted at some length:

> Various parameters operate when assessing whether a State has duly discharged the obligation concerned. The first, which varies greatly from one State to another, is clearly the capacity to influence effectively the action of persons likely to commit, or already committing, genocide. This capacity itself depends, among other things, on the geographic distance of the State concerned from the scene of the events, and on the strength of the political links, as well as links of all other kinds, between the authorities of that State and the main actors in the events. The State's capacity to influence must also be assessed by legal criteria, since it is clear that every State may only act within the limits permitted by international law; seen thus, a State's capacity to influence may vary depending on its particular legal position vis-à-vis the situations and persons facing the danger, or the reality, of the genocide. (par. 430)

After enunciating this test, the ICJ then applied this standard holding that, during the period under consideration, Serbia was in fact in a "position of influence" over the Bosnian Serbs "unlike that of any of the other States parties to the Genocide Convention owing to the strength of the political, military and financial links between the FRY on the one hand and the [Bosnian Serbs] on the other" (par. 434). Turning to the events at Srebrenica, the ICJ reiterated its position that the decision to eliminate physically the entire male adult population had not been brought to the attention of Serbian authorities before the fact.

> Nevertheless, given all the international concern about what looked likely to happen at Srebrenica . . . which made it clear that the dangers were known and that these dangers seemed to be of an order that could suggest intent to commit genocide, unless brought under control, it must have been clear that there was a serious risk of genocide in Srebrenica. Yet, the Respondent has not shown that it took any initiative to prevent what happened, or any action on its part to avert the atrocities which were committed. . . . As indicated above, for a State to be held responsible for breaching its obligation of prevention, it does not need to be proven that the State concerned definitely had the power to prevent genocide; it is sufficient that it had the means to do so and that it manifestly refrained from using them. (par. 438)

A few things need to be said about this part of the Court's holding. The first relates to the "influence" test created by the ICJ. While I see much merit to this standard, still, the Court never even begins to explain how and why there should be two completely different standards: an extraordinarily high "effective control" standard for determining state responsibility in situations of complicity and/or aiding and assisting, but then a fairly low "influence" standard for a state's unwillingness to work to "prevent" human rights abuses from taking place. What makes this odder still is that the "influence" standard is used for acts of omission (failure to prevent) but not for acts of commission (actually providing aid and assistance) while, if anything, a strong argument could be made for reversing these two things.

Another issue relates to the foreseeability of genocide and the ICJ's attempt to have things both ways. On the one hand, foreseeability apparently plays no role in the context of determining state responsibility for aiding and assisting in violations of human rights. In other words, a state that provides "aid and assistance" is not held responsible even if it was absolutely certain that this material was going to be used to carry out human rights violations (perhaps the receiving state informed the sending state of how its weapons would be put to use)—so long as the sending state did not exercise almost total control over how the receiving state used these weapons. Yet, foreseeability apparently does play (and should play) a key role in determining whether a state has met its duty to "prevent." As a side note to this, one of the questions that should be asked is whether genocide was all that "foreseeable," and the reason I say this is that if no acts of genocide had taken place before this (which is the Court's position), how and why would Serbian authorities have reason to know that Bosnian Serb forces would carry out genocide at Srebrenica?

Turning to the issue of "influence," there is no question of Serbia's "influence" over the various Bosnian Serb paramilitary groups—which, to reiterate my position, should also be a determining factor on the issue of state responsibility. However, what the Court never stops to consider is the kind of "influence" that other states (especially other European states) also possessed. In other words, if all state parties are "to employ all means reasonably available to them, so as to prevent genocide as far as possible" (par. 430), then a host of countries violated this standard as well. After all, there were a group of powerful states that might have taken much stronger diplomatic initiatives or engaged in military action in the face of genocide—yet, these states did virtually nothing. Furthermore, what is also odd is the Court's use of geographic proximity as a means of determining a state's "influence." Surely, a powerful country like the United States could have exerted all manner of "influence" over the Serbian government, even from across the ocean.

The final issue is whether Serbia had met its obligation to "punish" under the Genocide Convention. Article IV provides, "Persons committing genocide . . . shall be punished, whether they are constitutionally responsible rulers, public officials or private individuals," while Article VI reads, "Persons charged with genocide . . . shall be tried by a competent tribunal of the State in the territory of which the act was committed, or by such international tribunal as may have jurisdiction with respect to those Contracting Parties which shall have accepted its jurisdiction."

According to the Court's analysis, since the genocide in Srebrenica was not carried out on the Respondent state's territory, Serbia "cannot be charged with not having tried before its own courts those accused of having participated in the Srebrenica genocide, either as perpetrators or accomplices" (par. 442). In explaining this position, the ICJ held that, while Article VI does not prohibit states from conferring jurisdiction for trying extraterritorial acts of genocide, there is no legal obligation to do so. However, where the ICJ did find a violation was in Serbia's refusal to cooperate with the work of an "international penal tribunal," especially its apparent unwillingness to arrest General Mladić, one of those primarily responsible for the Srebrenica massacres.

There are several shortcomings to the Court's analysis that need to be pointed out and examined further. The first relates to the Court's rigid reading of Article VI. According to the ICJ, only the territorial state (Bosnia in this case) has a legal obligation to prosecute. While other states may be willing to prosecute, if they so choose, they are under no obligation to do so, and failure to do so does not constitute an internationally wrongful act. But isn't there something fundamentally wrong with a state party to the Genocide Convention not instituting any form of legal action against a person who directed and/or carried out acts of genocide who is within the territorial jurisdiction of that country?

In arriving at this conclusion the Court pretends that it is simply giving a literal reading to Article VI. But Article VI only makes mention of (1) courts in the territorial state and (2) an "international penal tribunal." Nowhere is there mention of courts or tribunals in other states. Thus, a literal reading of Article VI would actually prohibit any other state from instituting proceedings to "punish" those engaged in genocide. Again, I ask this question: is this really how the ICJ wishes to interpret the Genocide Convention?

PROSPECTS FOR CHANGE?

What we have seen thus far is how far removed the Law on State Responsibility is from assigning responsibility for engaging in practices that are destructive of human rights protection—at least as this relates to individuals living in foreign lands. To my mind, a more accurate term would be the Law on State or the Law on State Irresponsibility. Yet, not all of evidence is bad, and I want to focus on three possible developments. The first relates to the indictment of Liberia's Charles Taylor by the U.N.-backed Special Court for Sierra Leone. The indictment charges Taylor with "individual criminal responsibility" for crimes against humanity, war crimes, and other serious violations of international humanitarian law committed in Sierra Leone by rebel forces. As detailed in the indictment, Taylor's "responsibility" is based, at least in part, on the role he played in providing "financial support, military training, personnel, arms, ammunition and other support and encouragement" to rebel groups that committed massive levels of human rights violations. In other words, this part of the indictment is based on the notion that Charles Taylor committed a criminal act for what is essentially "aiding and assisting" those who violated human rights in another sovereign state (Misol 2004).

A second development has been the introduction of a proposal for an Arms Trade Treaty, which grew out of an initiative of Nobel Peace Laureates led by former Costa Rican president Oscar Arias. According to Article 3 of the "Draft Framework Convention on International Arms Transfers,"

> A Contracting Party shall not authorize international transfers of arms in circumstances in which it has knowledge or ought reasonably to have knowledge that transfers of arms of the kind under consideration are likely to be:
>
> a. used in breach of the United Nations Charter or corresponding rules or customary international law, in particular those on the prohibition on the threat or use of force in international relations;
> b. used in the commission of serious violations of human rights;
> c. used in the commission of serious violations of international humanitarian law applicable in international or non-international armed conflict;
> d. used in the commission of genocide or crimes against humanity;
> e. diverted and used in the commission of any of the acts referred to in the preceding sub-paragraphs of this Article.

The United Nations Special Rapporteur on Human Rights and Small Arms has explained the basis of the proposed treaty in these terms: "The Arms Trade Treaty proposes to limit State transfer of arms based on the anticipated use that will be made of the weapons by the recipient State. The exporting State's responsibility is based upon its international legal obligation not to participate in the wrongful acts of the recipient State" (Frey 2003, par. 57).

A third development comes from the "war on terror." In particular, what is interesting to note is the manner in which states (or at least Western states) are delineating "responsibility" for states that "aid and assist" terrorist organizations. Consider the American approach with respect to states that "sponsor" terrorism (Chase 2004). Under the Antiterrorism and Effective Death Penalty Act (AEDPA) of 1996, which amended the Foreign Sovereign Immunity Act, a state can be held civilly liable to a U.S. citizen for personal injury or death resulting from an act of torture, extrajudicial killing, aircraft sabotage, or hostage taking when the act "was either perpetrated by the foreign state directly or by a non-state actor which receives material support or resources from the foreign state defendant." In *Flatlow v. Islamic Republic of Iran* (1998), the family of a U.S. citizen who had been killed by a terrorist attack in Israel successfully brought suit against Iran for the "material support" that it had provided to a "terrorist" organization (the Shaqiqi faction of the Palestine Islamic Jihad). The U.S. State Department confirmed that the Iranian government had been providing approximately two million dollars each year to the Palestine Islamic Jihad. The court then proceeded to award a default judgment against Iran based on this "sponsorship" of this terrorist organization.

The real question is why such vastly disparate standards co-exist. In the context of fighting "terrorism," states are held to a fairly low standard, the idea being that sponsorship of terrorism is itself a legal "wrong" and, thus, such practices that "aid and assist" this wrong also have to be rooted out and eliminated. As noted before, under U.S. law, a state placed on the State Department's "State Sponsors of Terrorism List" will be held responsible for "aiding and assisting" a terrorist organization simply when it provides some form of "material support and resources" to this group. There is no requirement to show that this state had exercised any form of "effective control" or "overall control" over this terrorist organization or that its "intent" in providing support was to promote the cause of this organization specifically or of world terrorism more generally. This approach stands in stark contrast to the law on state responsibility, which has gone far in eliminating virtually all accountability and responsibility in situations of "aiding and assisting" states that perpetrate all other kinds of human rights violations.

STATE RESPONSIBILITY IN OTHER CONTEXTS

Transnational Corporations

States, guerrilla organizations, and terrorist cells do not have a monopoly on violating human rights. For all the good that they are able to bring about, transnational corporations (TNCs) have also been accused of bringing about enormous levels of harm in various places around the world, and here it has to be said that I am not speaking about such things as private mercenary organizations that states are increasingly relying on to fight wars for them (such as in Iraq) but rather about traditional corporate activities. David Kinley and Junko Tadaki provide a partial list of these abuses involving some of the world's leading corporations:

> Many TNCs, including Nike and The Gap, have been accused of violating their workers' rights to just and favorable conditions of work by paying unfair and inadequate wages, requiring unreasonable overtime, and providing unsafe working conditions. Furthermore, there is ample evidence of TNCs in suppressing trade unions and thereby denying workers the right to organize. It has been alleged, for instance, that Coca-Cola in Colombia and Phillips-Van Heusen in Guatemala have been associated with, or are directly responsible for, the systematic intimidation, torture, kidnapping, unlawful detention, and murder of trade-unionist employees by paramilitaries operating as both of these corporations' agents. TNCs in the extractive industries have caused environmental disasters, threatening the right to adequate food and the right to an adequate standard of living. Royal Dutch/Shell's oil production in Nigeria, and BHP Billiton's copper mining in Papua New Guinea, for example, seriously damaged the environment and the livelihood of peoples in local communities, which depended on fishing and farming. (Kinley and Tadaki 2004: 933)

In almost every situation, the problem has been the tremendous imbalance of power between the host state (especially Third World states) and many TNCs. In other words, many host states are too weak or too fearful that TNCs will pack up and move to another country to offer any kind of meaningful regulation. This, in turn, has resulted in the kinds of harms listed above. If regulation by the host state has not been the answer, international law has not provided much help either. Traditionally, international law has only regulated the behavior of states. Although international law has now been extended so as to include certain actions of individuals, it has not addressed abuses by TNCs in any kind of meaningful fashion. This is not to say that nothing has been done. International measures have included such well-meaning and high-sounding names as the Norms on the Responsibilities of Transnational Corporations and Other Business Enterprises with Regard to Human Rights; the Declaration on the Rights and Responsibilities of Individuals, Groups and Organs of Society to Promote and Protect

Universally Recognized Human Rights and Fundamental Freedoms; and, finally (and more simply), the U.N. Global Compact. However, not one of these proposals, declarations, and resolutions is legally binding. Thus, TNCs continue to have license to either carry out human rights violations themselves or to be complicit with others that do so.

The problem with the present approach is that it relies exclusively on the host state. Under this scheme, it is the host state—but only the host state—that has responsibility for guarding against violations committed by organizations that, by definition, are transnational or extraterritorial in scope. And if the host state is not able to offer such protection (and we know for a fact that there are many instances where this has been the case), we simply shrug our collective shoulders and walk away from this problem, but at the same time we seem genuinely puzzled that human rights are not taken more seriously.

It should be obvious that this approach to human rights has serious deficiencies. What it does is to place territorial limitations on what are supposed to be universal values. As I have stated before, this is not to question the principle that it is host state that has primary responsibility for protecting human rights within its own territorial borders. If a host state is able to do so, there simply is no reason to look any place else. However, the empirical evidence suggests that there are many instances where this has not been the case. My point is that there is no reason why we have to maintain a system that excludes all other states, thereby helping to perpetuate the commission of human rights violations.

In the present context, certainly the most obvious candidate (after the host state) for ensuring that a TNC is not violating human rights is the corporation's home state. Let me use the example of Nike, which has its world headquarters in Oregon. Nike has plants and factories in a number of developing countries, and in some of these it has been accused of violating workers' rights. The primary responsibility for protecting against such unlawful practices would be the various host states. Thus, with respect to Nike's operations in Vietnam, it is the Vietnamese government that has the primary responsibility for protecting workers' rights in that country.

The problem is that there is strong evidence that Vietnam is not doing this. Unfortunately, under our present approach to human rights this ends the matter—and human rights continue to be violated. But what about regulation by the United States? This question sounds odd only because it is widely, and almost naturally, assumed (even by many legal scholars) that a country's law and its legal remedies are limited by territorial considerations (Raustiala 2005). In other words, it is simply assumed that American law goes no further than the territorial boundaries of the United States. Yet, this is not true at all. When Nike operates a sneaker factory in Vietnam it continues to be regulated by a myriad of U.S. laws: American antitrust law, American monopoly law, American age discrimination law, American trademark law, American securities law, American civil rights law, and American bribery law—in addition, U.S. nationals working at this overseas operation are required by U.S. law to pay U.S. taxes. All that I am asking is whether Nike should not also be bound by American labor law and American health and safety law in the absence (or near absence) of such regulation by the Vietnamese government. Or to state this matter even more bluntly, shouldn't the U.S. government attempt to prevent one of its own corporations from violating human rights when it readily has the ability to do so?

I have no idea how or why or in what manner Nike decided to locate some of its manufacturing plants in Vietnam. However, the common image is that TNCs make their business decisions completely separate from the home state. Yet, home states have made it their business to aid and assist their own corporations. One observer describes this relationship between home states and "their" TNCs:

> Home state support for TNCs comes in a variety of forms. States negotiate bilateral and multilateral investment treaties that define the framework legal rights of TNCs; government export credit agencies offer overseas investment insurance to cover political risks, and in some cases commercial risks are borne by TNCs; and regional and national development finance institutions offer private sector financing. Politically, home states have played a role in the negotiation, rewriting, or enforcement of contracts that are heavily tilted in TNCs' favor. Home states have, for example, pushed developing countries to live up to "vastly unfair" contracts, even when those contracts were signed by corrupt host state officials who are no longer in power. The negotiating power of the TNC was, in these cases, fortified by the muscle power of the home state. (Narula 2006: 761, citations omitted)

One of the few proposals that have sought to regulate the overseas conduct of American TNCs was the Corporate Code of Conduct Act, which was (unsuccessfully) introduced as legislation before the Congress in 2000. The Act was designed to establish strict guidelines for

U.S.-based TNCs in terms of labor rights, human rights, and environmental protection based on American and internationally recognized standards. The Act would apply to any U.S. national that "employs more than 20 persons in a foreign country, either directly or indirectly through subsidiaries, subcontractors, affiliates, joint ventures, partners or licensees," and it set forth rewards for compliance through preference on government contracts but also punishment for noncompliance through the withdrawal of taxpayer-financed assistance and liability under U.S. courts. In particular, the Act established that, in their overseas operations, American TNCs would

1. provide a safe and healthy workplace;
2. ensure fair employment, including prohibition on the use of child and forced labor, prohibition of discrimination based upon race, gender, national origin, or religious beliefs, respect for freedom of association and the right to organize independently and bargain collectively, and the payment of a living wage to all workers;
3. prohibit mandatory overtime work by employees under 18;
4. prohibit the practice of pregnancy testing of employees, forced usage of birth control, and dismissal or discrimination of employees based on pregnancy;
5. prohibit retaliation against any employee who conveys information relating to a violation or alleged violation of any fair employment requirement of this code;
6. promote specified good governance and good business practices;
7. maintain a corporate culture that respects free expression consistent with the workplace, encourages good corporate citizenship, makes a positive contribution to the communities in which the U.S. national operates, and promotes ethical conduct by all employees;
8. comply with internationally recognized worker rights and core labor standards;
9. uphold responsible environmental protection standards;
10. require partners, suppliers, and subcontractors of the U.S national government (including any security forces) to adopt and adhere to these principles;
11. require full public disclosure of specified information; and
12. implement and monitor compliance with these principles through a self-financing program internal to the business that meets specified requirements. (Borg 2003: 626–27)

Using U.S. law to regulate the egregious behavior by American corporations should not seem revolutionary, but apparently it is. But I think it is important to push this even further so that a state (and not just the United States) that does *not* regulate one of its own TNCs will be held "responsible" under international law for its failure to do so. In other words, if the French government knows (or should know) that Michelin is carrying out human rights abuses in other countries (or is complicit in such) but the French government does not do anything about this, then the French government itself has committed an international wrong. It should be noted that this is completely consistent with the Maastricht Guidelines on Violations of Economic, Social and Cultural Rights, which are an influential source of guidance in terms of the implementation of the Economic Covenant. Guideline 18 reads as follows:

> The obligation to protect includes the State's responsibility to ensure that private entities or individuals, including transnational corporations over which they exercise jurisdiction, do not deprive individuals of their economic, social and cultural rights. States are responsible for violations of economic, social and cultural rights that result from their failure to exercise due diligence in controlling the behaviour of such non-state actors.

To summarize, what I am arguing is that, when Nike is doing business in Vietnam, the Vietnamese government has the primary responsibility for protecting the human rights of its own citizens (as well as the human rights of foreign nationals living in that country, including American employees). If, however, the Vietnamese government fails to do this, then the task of protecting these "universal" human rights falls to other states, all of which have a secondary responsibility. Of all these "other" states, the country that would seem to have the greatest ability and interest (and obligation) in regulating the human rights practices of this TNC is the home country. Perhaps U.S. law is somehow unique, but home countries continue to have an enormous influence on their TNCs, wherever they are doing business. The point is that when an American corporation (like Nike) violates the human rights of people in other countries (such as Vietnam), this also constitutes a failure on the part of the United States. U.S. law could easily help to guard against these violations, but it does not. Thus, in my view, the United States is committing an internationally wrongful act—it is itself violating human rights—through its failure to protect human rights when it readily could do so.

But the United States is not the only country that has done wrong. Nike does business in places all over the globe. The problem, however, is that states apparently only look at how a corporation acts within its own territory—but no place else. Thus, while the German government is mighty interested in how Nike operates on German soil, apparently it is completely disinterested in what Nike does any place else (such as Vietnam). Thus, the German state (as well as every other state) does not see it as its own responsibility for doing anything about the human rights problems caused by Nike's operations in Vietnam. Rather, the dominant (if not universal) view is that this is Vietnam's problem—but only Vietnam's problem.

But shouldn't Germany have some interest in what Nike is doing in Vietnam? After all, Germany is a state party to practically every international human rights treaty in existence. In each one of these conventions the German government and the German people have pledged themselves to protect human rights—in Germany, for sure, but in other places in the world as well. Moreover, one of the entities that have been accused of committing human rights violations happens to be doing business—in Germany! Is it so strange, then, to think that the German government might use its (considerable) leverage to try to address this issue? I understand that this idea will sound strange. But so does the opposite idea. This would be like saying that a Cambodian war criminal is not a war criminal in France simply because he has not carried out any war crimes in that country. We would reject this idea outright and insist that France engage in legal proceedings against this person. Yet, for some reason, this is how states approach the question of corporate harms.

What international law needs to do is to spell out the responsibilities of states (primary and secondary alike) and it needs to do so in a manner that is vastly more subtle, more nuanced—and certainly more "responsible"—than any of the various tests that have been thrown around so loosely and so ineffectively. We will end this discussion by looking briefly at the *Trail Smelter* decision (1941), one of the earliest (and greatest) cases dealing with state responsibility and corporate harm. The case involved a situation where fumes from private smelter plants located in Canada were causing environmental harm in the United

States. The United States responded by bringing a claim against Canada before a special international tribunal, and this body held that Canada was in violation of international law: "Under the principles of international law . . . no State has the right to use or permit the use of its territory in such a manner as to cause injury by fumes in or to the territory of another or the properties or persons therein, when the case is of serious consequence and the injury is established by clear and convincing evidence."

Trail Smelter can be read one of two ways. The first would be to limit its holding to the particular factual situation of that case: a state will be responsible under international law when one of its own corporations—physically situated within that country—causes environmental harm in another state. However, the second way to interpret the rule of law in this case is to see this as creating a general duty on the part of states to help ensure that their corporations—wherever they might be located—do not cause harm (and not simply environmental harm) to other people. To my mind, the second interpretation is vastly superior and certainly more in line with why international human rights law (as well as international environmental law) exists in the first place.

International Organizations

There has been an increasing amount of attention lately to the human rights obligations of international organizations, most notably, the World Bank and the International Monetary Fund. There are two assumptions at work here, neither of which happens to be true. The first is that international organizations have always been bound by international law. The second is that international organizations have always protected human rights.

In terms of the first issue, it was only recently that the International Law Commission decided to include the topic of "Responsibility of international organizations" in its long-term work program (Suzuki and Nanwani 2005). For a long time international organizations fought against the idea that they had obligations under international human rights law.

The second assumption has also not been true. One of the leading authorities in this field, Dana Clark, offers this summary of the kinds of human rights violations the World Bank has been accused of being complicit in:

At the country level, the disproportionate impacts of Bank-supported structural adjustment policies on the poorest sectors of society have often been cited as undermining, if not violating, economic and social rights, as well as subverting the Bank's overall development mission. The Bank's history of involvement with involuntary resettlement has been a well-documented failure, resulting in forcible impoverishment of displaced communities and having particularly severe impacts on indigenous peoples and ethnic minorities. The Bank is frequently criticized for providing financial backing and an aura of legitimacy to regimes that are known to have committed serious violations of human rights or that have a reputation for corruption. (Clark 2002: 206, citations omitted)

In response to these kinds of accusations, in 1993 the World Bank created an Inspection Panel through which individuals who claim to be harmed by a World Bank–financed project could file a claim against the Bank. In some respects, these Inspection Panels have proven to be successful. If nothing else, this represents an advance over the old order where individuals who were negatively affected by a World Bank project—perhaps one of the millions of people displaced by a dam project that had been financed by the Bank—had absolutely no recourse. Since then, this idea of self-monitoring has spread to other international (and regional) financial institutions, although it is noteworthy that the International Monetary Fund continues to resist this idea.

Yet, what also has to be said is how timid and meager the Inspections Panel concept has been. Most importantly, claims are limited to the sole question of whether the Bank followed its own internal procedures or not. If the World Bank did so—but the project was an unmitigated disaster in the sense that it resulted in massive levels of human rights violations—victims simply have no claim.

A much better approach would be to focus on violations of human rights—not violations of internal operating procedures—and to assign legal responsibility to states themselves. One way of doing this is by consigning legal responsibility according to voting weight. Thus, if France has 10 percent of the vote in the World Bank and votes in favor of a project that causes massive levels of human rights violations, the French government should bear 10 percent of the responsibility for these wrongs.

MAKING THE LAW ON STATE RESPONSIBILITY RESPONSIBLE

We live in a world marked by massive levels of human rights violations, and one of the primary reasons for this is that international law has failed miserably in recognizing the various levels of responsibility for these violations—that is, international human rights law has had enormous difficulty getting beyond the notion of primary responsibility, thereby ignoring the manner in which other states and other institutions "aid and assist" in helping to perpetuate many of these violations.

This is not meant to suggest that a state that arms and equips a murderous regime can never be held accountable for its actions. However, the law on state responsibility seems far more intent in protecting states than in protecting human rights. What we have examined in this chapter are the various tests and standards that have been developed in order to determine whether a state that "aids or assists" an entity that violates human rights directly bears any legal responsibility for doing so. There is the "effective control" test from the International Court of Justice decisions in *Nicaragua* and *Bosnia*, which for all practical purposes translates into an "absolute control" standard. Thus, states that provide aid and assistance to another state or to an entity in another state (such as an insurgency group) will only be held "responsible" in those exceedingly rare instances where the sending state exercises near total control over the receiving state/entity. The International Criminal Tribunal for the Former Yugoslavia has rejected the ICJ's "effective control" test and employed its own "overall control" standard. We also examined the work of the International Law Commission and the way in which its Articles on State Responsibility demand that a sponsoring state must know not only that the entity that its supports is violating international law but also that its "intent" in providing this support was to achieve this very end. The sum of these tests is that "sending" states bear almost no responsibility under international law. The law on state responsibility assigns no responsibility at all.

There is, however, at least some indication of hope, as slight as this might be. One such measure is the proposed Arms Trade Treaty, which would hold states responsible for shipping arms to human rights–abusing entities when these "sending" states know or should know that their weapons will be used to violate human rights. Another noteworthy development, or at least what should be a noteworthy development, is the manner in which Western states have employed a very low threshold in the realm of "international terrorism" by holding states "responsible" for providing virtually any form of material assistance to any terrorist organization.

My own view is that the law on state responsibility should look something very close to the notion of "responsibility" in the context of the war on terrorism. The reason states pursue countries that "aid and assist" terrorist organizations is really quite simple: terrorism is wrong, and states that "aid and assist" such wrongs are themselves committing a "legal wrong." But the real question is why this same standard should not apply in the context of human rights. A state that carries out certain actions (or refuses to take action when it has a legal obligation to do so) with full knowledge that this will work toward the destruction of human rights protection should bear *some* degree of responsibility for the harms that ensue. In order to explore this issue further, I will close this chapter by looking at a number of real-world scenarios, several of which occurred during the time this chapter was being written. I will also return to the hypothetical in the introduction, which, unfortunately, in the real world is not hypothetical enough.

Western Trade Barriers

At the present time, Western states spend approximately one billion dollars per day on subsidies to protect their own farmers (Watkins and Fowler 2002). The most nefarious consequence of this is that these trade barriers help to keep Third World goods out of Western markets, which has the effect of further impoverishing poor farmers in poor countries. During the summer of 2006, there were trade talks scheduled to address this issue, but they eventually collapsed and nothing was done (Weisman and Barionuevo 2006). Thus, Western states—the same group that constantly hectors Third World states about free trade—have pursued a policy that (1) goes directly against the principle of free trade but, more importantly, (2) has helped perpetuate massive levels of human rights violations (Vandenhole 2007).

The first problem is that we refuse to recognize this as a human rights issue, viewing it instead in terms of trade or macroeconomics. Granted, there is no actual blood on the collective hands of the Western trade ministers. Yet, there is no question (not even Western officials dispute this) that these policies have had a devastating effect in terms of the continued deprivation of economic rights in Third World states. At the end of the day there is a conflict between the needs of domestic (Western) farmers and the human rights of people in other countries—and the former wins every time. And one of the primary reasons for this is that we allow ourselves to take such a narrow (and self-serving) view of what constitutes state responsibility for violating human rights.

Two things need to be changed. The first is to recognize the human rights aspect of these trade restrictions. The second is that the law on state responsibility has to be changed so that it reflects degrees of responsibility. A far better test than "control" or "intent" is the degree to which a state's actions (or inactions) help to destroy human rights protection. The point is that by maintaining trade barriers that prevent Third World goods from entering their markets, Western states are taking actions that help to violate human rights—and international law must recognize this.

Cluster Bombs

A second example that also arose during the summer of 2006 involves Israel's invasion of southern Lebanon to fight Hezbollah insurgents. The particular issue I want to focus on is Israel's use of American-made cluster bombs. What came to light after the fighting ended was that, in deploying these weapons against civilian populations, Israel had violated a secret agreement with the United States from whom it had purchased these weapons (Cloud and Myre 2007).

Little is known about the arrangement between the two countries. However, according to press reports, these restrictions require that these munitions only be used against organized armies and clearly defined military targets. A congressional investigation conducted after Israel's 1982 invasion of Lebanon found that American-made cluster bombs had been used against civilian populations. In response, the Reagan administration then imposed a six-year ban on further sales to Israel, although American shipments apparently resumed some time after this.

Even less is known about what is behind U.S. policy. Are these restrictions an indication that the United States believes that, in using cluster bombs against civilian populations, Israel is committing war crimes and the United States is concerned with being complicit in these crimes? Or are these restrictions simply an attempt to score some political points with Arab states and Arab populations? The answer is not clear.

But this leads to this question concerning the 2006 war: should the United States bear some degree of "responsibility" for the human rights and humanitarian law violations caused by Israel's use of these bombs? I believe the evidence is mixed. On the one hand, the United States has attempted to limit Israel's use of such weapons, and it is noteworthy for purposes of attributing responsibility on this matter that the United States had previously suspended shipment when there was evidence that Israel had used these weapons in a situation (Lebanon) that the United States had prohibited. On the other hand, it could be argued that the United States was already on notice that Israel was quite capable of ignoring such restrictions and yet it persisted in selling these weapons with full knowledge of this.

My own view from what little is known is that the United States would/should bear some responsibility, but far less than it would/should have if it had not made any attempt to exercise some measure of control over how Israel used such weapons. What would also help to determine responsibility is what the United States does now. Will it continue to sell cluster bombs to Israel, with full knowledge of how Israel has used these weapons—once again? Or will the United States cut off the sale of such weapons, as it did in the 1980s? The larger point is that state responsibility should be based on degrees of responsibility.

The Mexico City Policy and Health Care in Kenya

A recent report from the Crowley Program in International Human Rights at Fordham Law School raises a number of issues that are quite pertinent to our present discussion. The purpose of the study was to empirically examine the effects of the "Global Gag Order" (better known as the Mexico City Policy) on the enjoyment of health in a country (Kenya) that had been receiving funding from the U.S. Agency for International Development (USAID).

By way of some background, the Mexico City Policy is an Executive Memorandum that was issued by President George W. Bush on January

22, 2001, that reinstated a set of restrictions prohibiting foreign non-governmental recipients of U.S. family planning funds from promoting or advocating abortion as a means of family planning, in situations other than that of protecting a woman's health. These restrictions bind USAID, the principal conduit through which U.S. funding for health care is provided to Kenya and in other developing states. At the time that the "Global Gag Rule" was issued, USAID provided 16 percent of all health care funding to Kenya and 28.4 percent of the Ministry of Health's development budget.

The Fordham study focused on two Kenyan family planning organizations (Maria Stopes International-Kenya and Family Planning Association of Kenya), both of which refused to sign the required pledge not to "perform or actively promote abortion." USAID responded by cutting off funding. Due to ensuing budgetary shortfalls, both organizations found it necessary to close down a number of their family planning clinics and outreach programs. The end result of all this is that the number of Kenyans receiving family planning services has been significantly reduced, and there are already indications of a serious deterioration in the level of health (particularly maternal health) in Kenya. Or to make this even more basic: there has been a sharp increase in violations of the "right to health" in Kenya.

The question to be asked is this: is the United States "responsible" for this increase in death and suffering? Has the United States committed an internationally wrongful act when it cut off funding to these family planning clinics in Kenya? Under the dominant approach to international law, the United States would not be responsible. For one thing, many still cling to the idea that there is a difference between acts and non-acts. An "act" would be something like torturing a person. On the other hand, cutting off funding would be viewed by many as not constituting an "action" as such. Another rationale that would be relied upon (and one that we will explore more fully in the next chapter) would be that whatever human rights obligations the United States possesses, these are only applicable to domestic practices, not international or extraterritorial practices. Of course, what would make this argument even stronger is the fact that, while the United States has signed the Economic Covenant (where the right to health is most clearly protected), it has never ratified this treaty. Finally, and to get away from international human rights law altogether, at least for a moment, I am quite confident that there would be a general "feeling" that, after all, this is American money—and, as such, the U.S. government can do whatever it wants with it.

These are all solid arguments, and I do not mean to discount or dismiss any of them. However, what cannot be denied is the extraordinarily close cause and effect relationship between the actions of the American government and the increase in human suffering in Kenya. We would have little trouble understanding and accepting the notion of U.S. "responsibility" if American warplanes dropped bombs on Kenya, thereby killing thousands of individuals. However, we have much more difficulty in thinking about "responsibility" in situations such as the present one. Still, my own view is in accordance with the authors of the study:

> Holding Kenya responsible for the effects of a policy instituted by the United States may appear beside the point in any setting other than international law. As this report notes, Kenya has assumed binding obligations to realize the right to health, the elimination of discrimination based upon gender, and freedom of expression. As this Report further documents, the impact of the Mexico City restrictions within the country suggest that, in the first instance, the Kenyan government has failed to make good on these legal obligations. This legal conclusion, however, begs the practical reality. But for the Mexico City Policy, the reductions in health and reproductive care, disproportionate impact on women, and attempted censorship of reproductive medical information described here would not have occurred. This is not to say that the Kenyan government was powerless to anticipate and mitigate these effects. Yet, at the end of the day, the effective causes for the challenges under review comprise the funding restrictions, USAID, and the United States. (Hoodbhoy et al. 2005: 91–92, citations omitted)

Rwandan Genocide

The last scenario involves the horrific 1994 genocide in Rwanda during which time approximately 800,000 people were killed. The first thing to note is that this ethnic conflict between Hutus and Tutsis did not suddenly arise out of nowhere. Instead, there already had been several outbreaks of massive violence in previous years. But what also has to be noted is that these episodes in no way dissuaded Western countries from continuing to sell any and all weapons to the warring factions that they could. According to a Human Rights Watch study, some of the worst offenders in this regard were France, South Africa, Israel, and Albania (Misol 2004).

The second thing to point out is also not widely disputed, namely, that after the genocide began in 1994 Western states not only did not intervene, but they actually took measures to prevent African states from intervening as well (Gourevitch 1998). Ultimately, one of these states (France) did intervene, but its intervention was aimed at protecting its former Hutu ally—the group responsible for carrying out this genocide.

The 1994 Rwandan genocide so often serves as a poster child for man's inhumanity to man. However, the only inhumanity we are capable of recognizing is that between Hutus and Tutsis. What we refuse to acknowledge is our own inhumanity in any of this—or any responsibility under international law. The Genocide Convention was one of the international community's first responses to the horrors of the Holocaust. Under Article 1, state parties pledge themselves (legally) to "prevent and to punish" those who carry out genocide. For decades, states understood this language as obligating them to "do something" when genocide occurred—which is the reason states have systematically avoided ever (or almost ever) using the word "genocide" to describe actual genocide.

One of the belated responses of the international community to the Rwandan genocide was the creation of the International Criminal Tribunal for Rwanda (ICTR), which has initiated prosecution against some of the most egregious offenders—all Rwandan. What I am suggesting is that "responsibility" for these genocidal horrors does not reside solely in the Hutu population of Rwanda or even among Rwandans themselves. Rather, there are a number of states and international institutions such as the United Nations that are also responsible—morally *and* legally. First of all, there are the states that sold arms and equipment to Rwanda before the genocide. Second, there are the states that not only refused to intervene but also actively worked to prevent other states (particularly African states) from intervening. Finally, the French authorities (and the French state) should be held accountable for the shameful way that it intervened on behalf of the *genocidaires*.

RETURNING TO THE HYPOTHETICAL

You might recall the hypothetical situation I posited in the introduction. In it, State A carried out torture while all of the other states did various things that "aided and assisted" State A. State B sends torture equipment to State A; State C trains State A's torturers; State D allows State A to use its territory to carry out torture; State E tortures citizens of State A under State A's direction; State F refuses to either "prosecute or extradite" torturers of State A who were within its territorial jurisdiction; State G has instituted visa restrictions that prevents State A's citizens (who are would-be refugee claimants) from being able to flee to State G; State H rejects all asylum claims from citizens of State A; State I refuses to issue an inter-state complaint against State A; and, finally, State J and State K grant sovereign immunity protection to State A.

It is clear that State A violates international human rights law. Yet, what can be said about the actions of each of these other countries? Unfortunately and inexplicably enough, it is not clear that any one of these other countries has committed an internationally wrongful act (the closest, I believe, would be State E). In light of this, let me close this chapter by asking this question: is international law really all that serious about protecting human rights?

REFERENCES

Antiterrorism and Effective Death Penalty Act [AEDPA]. 22 U.S.C. Sec. 2377-2378 (2004).

Borg, Erin. 2003. "Sharing the Blame for September Eleventh: The Case for a New Law to Regulate the Activities of American Corporations Abroad." *Arizona Journal of International and Comparative Law* 20:607–43.

Case Concerning Military and Paramilitary Activities in and against Nicaragua (Nicaragua v. United States). 1986 I.C.J. 14.

Chase, Alison Elizabeth. 2004. "Legal Mechanisms of the International Community and the United States Concerning State Sponsorship of Terrorism." *Virginia Journal of International Law* 45:41–137.

Clark, Dana. 2002. "The World Bank and Human Rights: The Need for Greater Accountability." *Harvard Human Rights Journal* 15:205–26.

Cloud, David S., and Greg Myre. 2007. "Israel May Have Violated Arms Pact, U.S. Officials Say." *New York Times*, January 28, A3.

Crawford, James. 2002. *The International Law Commission's Articles on State Responsibility: Introduction, Text and Commentaries.* Cambridge, UK: Cambridge University Press.

Flatlow v. Islamic Republic of Iran. 999 F. Supp. 1 (D.D.C. 1998).

Foreign Sovereign Immunity Act [FSIA]. 28 U.S.C. 1602-1611 (2004).

Frey, Barbara. 2003. *Preliminary Report on the Prevention of Human Rights Violations Committed with Small Arms and Light Weapons.* E/CN.4/Sub.2/2003/29 (June 25).

Gibney, Mark, Katarina Tomasevski, and Jens Vedsted-Hansen. 1999. "Transnational State Responsibility for Violations of Human Rights." *Harvard Human Rights Journal* 12:267–96.

Gourevitch, Philip. 1998. *We Wish to Inform You That Tomorrow We Will Be Killed with Our Families: Stories from Rwanda.* New York: Farrar, Straus and Giroux.

Hoodbhoy, Mehlika, Martin S. Flaherty, and Tracy E. Higgins. 2005. "Exporting Despair: The Human Rights Implications of U.S. Restrictions on Foreign Health Care Funding in Kenya." *Fordham International Law Journal* 29:1–118.

Kinley, David, and Junko Tadaki. 2004. "From Talk to Walk: The Emergence of Human Rights Responsibilities for Corporations at International Law." *Virginia Journal of International Law* 44:931–1023.

"Limburg Principles on the Implementation of the International Covenant on Economic, Social and Cultural Rights." 1987. *Human Rights Quarterly* 9:122–35.

Misol, Lisa. 2004. "Weapons and War Crimes: The Complicity of Arms Suppliers." Human Rights Watch, at http://hrw.org/wr2k4/13.htm

Nahapetian, Kate. 2002. "Confronting State Complicity in International Law." *UCLA Journal of International and Foreign Affairs* 7:99–127.

Narula, Smita. 2006. "The Right to Food: Holding Global Actors Accountable under International Law." *Columbia Journal of Transnational Law* 44:691–800.

Prosecutor v. Tadic (Judgment). Case No. IT-94-1-A, 38 I.L.M. 1518 (1999).

Raustiala, Kal. 2005. "The Geography of Justice." *Fordham Law Review* 73:2501–60.

Suzuki, Eisuke, and Suresh Nanwani. 2005. "Responsibility of International Organizations: The Accountability Mechanism of Multilateral Development Banks." *Michigan Journal of International Law* 27:177–225.

Trail Smelter Case (U.S. v. Canada). 3 R.I.A.A. 1905 (1941).

Vandenhole, Wouter. 2007. "Third State Obligations under the ICESCR: A Case Study of EU Sugar Policy." *Nordic Journal of International Law* 76:71–98.

Watkins, Kevin, and Penny Fowler. 2002. *Rigged Rules and Double Standards: Trade Globalisation, and the Fight against Poverty.* Oxford: Oxfam.

Weisman, Steven R., and Alexei Barionuevo. 2006. "Failure of Global Trade Talks Is Traced to the Power of Farmers." *New York Times*, July 27, C1.

STEP TWO:
TERRITORY

In the previous chapter we examined the law on state responsibility, and our focus there was on what behavior constituted an international wrong. What we found, unfortunately but perhaps predictably enough, is that international law has concerned itself almost exclusively with the state that actually carries out a wrong—while states that "aid and assist" this outlaw state will seldom, if ever, bear any legal responsibility for their own actions.

In this chapter we focus not so much on the nature of state behavior but on where this behavior takes place. To state matters bluntly, Western countries have come to work under the assumption that their obligations under international human rights treaties extend no further than their own territorial borders. What is particularly troubling about this is that these states believe this to be true not only with respect to positive obligations, or the obligation to provide assistance, but also with respect to negative obligations, or the obligation not to cause harm. Thus, while Western states apparently feel bound by the provisions of international human rights law when acting within their own domestic realm, these countries have universally rejected the idea that these same restrictions apply when they are acting in the international realm. A less elegant way of phrasing this would be to say that Western states operate under the assumption that they can "do" things outside their own territory that they are prohibited from doing at home, and at least two of the world's leading judicial bodies (the United States Supreme Court and the European Court of Human

Rights) have given these states license to do just that. Of course, no court would ever announce that states are now free to violate human rights as long as this is done outside their territorial borders. However, as we will see, this is exactly where decisions of these two leading judicial bodies lead to.

This story is told in three parts using three different judicial episodes. The first involves a challenge to the legality of the Haitian interdiction program, which involved U.S. Coast Guard boats stopping rafts fleeing from Haiti on the high seas and "returning" these individuals back to this troubled and violent country. The second concerns whether the European Convention protects people living outside of "Europe" from the harmful actions of European states. The final section of this chapter focuses on the American "war on terror" and the role that "territory" (as well as issues of "state responsibility") has played in this realm.

What we will find in this chapter is that Western states have a dedication to the notion of "territory"—or at least their own territory—that has at times proven to be destructive of human rights protection. What is never seriously questioned is the ability of Western states to act outside their borders in the first place, whether it is intercepting ships on the high seas or dropping bombs on civilian populations in a foreign land or holding foreign nationals in military bases, and so on. The lawfulness of these extraterritorial actions is simply assumed. Rather, the only thing being questioned is whether Western states are still bound by any international or regional human rights treaties when they do act outside their borders. These states maintain that they are not, and this answer has generally been confirmed by various judicial bodies.

I will argue that this position is wrong and that states must not be allowed to discard their human rights obligations in this manner. This notion of "territory" has been destructive of human rights protection in at least two ways. The first is the most obvious, and it relates to foreign nationals who have been killed or harmed by and through the actions of Western actors. Beyond this, however, the hypocrisy of Western states is most assuredly not lost on non-Western states. How and why would Western states think that they can lecture non-Western states on the latter's human rights practices when the West takes such a narrow and self-serving approach to human rights?

DENYING HUMAN RIGHTS PROTECTION ON THE HIGH SEAS

The issue before the U.S. Supreme Court in *Sale v. Haitian Centers Council* (1993) was whether the U.S. Coast Guard's Haitian interdiction program was in violation of either U.S. domestic law or international law. The Court ruled that neither law was applicable to American activities on the high seas.

By way of some background, on September 23, 1981, the United States and the Republic of Haiti entered into an agreement authorizing the U.S. Coast Guard to intercept vessels thought to be engaged in the illegal transportation of undocumented aliens to the United States. Although the two state parties agreed to prosecute "illegal traffickers," the Haitian government guaranteed that it would not punish repatriated citizens for their illegal departure. For its part, the U.S. government agreed that it would not return any passengers "whom the United States authorities determine[d] to qualify for refugee status."

A few days later (September 29), President Ronald Reagan issued an Executive Order that characterized this issue as a "serious national security problem detrimental to the interests of the United States." However, the Order expressly provided that "no person who is a refugee will be returned without his consent." Over the course of the next decade, the Coast Guard interdicted and interviewed approximately 25,000 Haitian migrants. Yet, notwithstanding the incredible levels of violence afflicting Haiti at that time, of the 22,716 boatpeople who were interviewed, only twenty-eight (that is not a misprint) were deemed to have made a credible showing of political refugee status and were allowed to be transported to the United States in order to file a formal application for asylum. All of the rest were returned to Haiti.

A decade later almost to the day (September 30, 1991), a group of military leaders removed the head of the Haitian government (Jean Bertrand Aristide), the first democratically elected president in Haitian history. What ensued immediately was societal-wide violence, including widespread killings, torture, and illegal detentions. In response to this, the Coast Guard suspended repatriations for a period of several weeks, and the United States imposed sanctions on Haiti. However, on November 18, 1991, the Coast Guard announced the resumption of the Haitian interdiction program and along with that forced repatriation. During the six-month period following October 1991, the Coast Guard interdicted over 34,000 Haitians. In an attempt to deal with this flow, the Department of Defense established temporary facilities at the U.S. Naval Base at Guantanamo, Cuba. However, this facility reached its capacity within a short period of time.

According to the Supreme Court's own interpretation of events, the Bush administration was thereby faced with one of two options: to either allow Haitians into the United States for this screening process or else to repatriate all Haitians without the benefit of any hearing whatsoever. The Bush administration (and later the Clinton administration) chose the latter option. It was this policy that was at issue in the *Sale* case.

There are two statutory provisions that are pertinent to our present discussion, one from U.S. domestic law (Sec. 243 [h] [1] of the Immigration and Nationality Act) and one from international law (Article 33 of the Refugee Convention). Section 243 (h) (1) reads as follows: "The Attorney General shall not deport or return any alien . . . to a country if the Attorney General determines that such alien's life or freedom would be threatened in such country on account of race, religion, nationality, membership in a particular social group, or political opinion."

It is important to note that the original version of this bill read much differently. Prior to 1980, the Attorney General was authorized "to withhold deportation of any alien . . . *within the United States* in which in his opinion the alien would be subject to persecution." One change in the law, then, was to eliminate the requirement that, in order to receive protection under the withholding statute, the alien had to be physically present in this country. The second change brought about by passage of the 1980 Refugee Act was that the Attorney General was not only barred from "deporting" aliens but also from "returning" an alien whose life or freedom would be threatened. Finally, the third change is that the prohibition against deporting or returning an individual to a country where her or his life or freedom "would be threatened" was now made mandatory, thus eliminating the Attorney General's discretion over such decisions.

The Court's analysis of these changes consisted of equal parts evasion and obfuscation. For one thing, the majority opinion (this was an 8-1 decision) gave almost no weight to the elimination of the explicit territorial restrictions that had been in the law prior to 1980. What is so terribly odd about this is that this very question of the scope of Section 243 (h) goes to the heart of the question before the Court. In terms of the second change, the addition of the word "return," the Court held that this was simply intended to cover both exclusionary hearings as well as deportation hearings—but that it was never intended to address aliens who were some distance away from the United States. Finally, with respect to the fact that withholding was made mandatory after 1980, the Court quickly dispatched this issue by holding that the law (mandatory or not) had no application to aliens situated on the high seas.

It is widely accepted that the 1980 Refugee Act sought to conform U.S. obligations under the United Nations Convention relating to the Status of Refugees (Refugee Convention), which the United States had ratified in 1968. The most important provision of the Refugee Act is its nonrefoulement provision in Article 33, which provides the following:

Article 33 Prohibition of expulsion or return ("refoulement")

1. No Contracting State shall expel or return ("refouler") a refugee in any manner whatsoever to the frontiers of territories where his life or freedom would be threatened on account of his race, religion, nationality, membership of a particular social group or political opinion.
2. The benefit of the present provision may not, however, be claimed by a refugee whom there are reasonable grounds for regarding as a danger to the security of the country in which he is, or who, having been convicted by a final judgment of a particularly serious crime, constitutes a danger to the community of that country.

The Court presented two arguments in support of its conclusion that Article 33 was without extraterritorial effect. The first is a rather convoluted (and unconvincing) argument, and it relates to the relationship between Paragraphs 1 and 2. I will let the Court try to explain its position for itself:

If the first paragraph did apply on the high seas, no nation could invoke the second paragraph's exception with respect to an alien there: An alien intercepted on the high seas is in no country at all. If Article 33.1 applied extraterritorially, therefore, Article 33.2 would create an absurd anomaly: Dangerous aliens on the high seas would be entitled to the benefits of 33.1, while those residing in the country that sought to expel them would not. It is more reasonable to assume that the coverage of 33.2 was limited to those already in the country, because it was understood that 33.1 obligated the signatory state only with respect to aliens within its territory.

As the dissent rightly points out, far from creating an "absurd anomaly," the fact that the Refugee Convention allows states to expel or remove a small number of dangerous refugees found within their territory is perfectly consonant with the overall aim of the Convention itself—and in no way should this be used as a means of removing human rights protections from *all* those who are seeking asylum but who are not (yet) within the receiving state's territorial borders. What is a much greater "absurd anomaly" is interpreting the Refugee Convention in a way that leaves no protection to the very people the treaty was intended to protect.

But to return to the Court's analysis, the real crux of the majority's opinion rests with its interpretation of the word "return," a term that is used in both Section 243 (h) and Article 33. According to the Court, when the U.S. Coast Guard would stop vessels on the high seas and then bring these passengers back to Haiti, it was not effectuating a "return"— or at least not a return in a legal sense.

According to the Court, "return" is a defensive act of resistance and it means to "repulse" rather than to "reinstate." This is an acceptable interpretation, particularly in light of the inclusion of the French word "refouler" in the Convention language. However, in the Court's opinion a "return" can only be effectuated at a state's territorial borders—but not before then. Thus, if one of these Haitian rafts was stopped right at the American border, bringing this boat and its inhabitants back to Haiti would be a "return" and the Attorney General would be obligated under both domestic and international law not to send this person back to Haiti if she or he determined that this person's life or freedom would be threatened. However, if the boat was, say, 100 feet off the shoreline, bringing this ship back would not be a "return," and none of the protections of Section 243 (h) would apply.

The Court believed there was support for this position in the drafting history of the Refugee Convention. It made note of the fact that during one of the negotiating sessions the Swiss delegate had stated that it was his country's understanding that "return" or "expel" referred only to refugees who had already entered the host country. In a subsequent meeting, the Dutch delegate made reference to these earlier remarks and commented that there was a "general consensus" behind this interpretation. For the Court, this expression of a "general consensus"— made by a single delegate!—was good enough evidence of the existence of an actual general consensus. Furthermore, the Court pointed out that there was "no record of any later disagreement with this position."

Sale was an 8-1 decision, with the lone dissent being filed by Justice Blackmun. In Blackmun's view, the language of Article 33.1 is unambiguous and it settles the matter completely: "Vulnerable refugees shall not be returned. The language is clear, and the command is straightforward: that should be the end of the inquiry." 509 U.S. at 190.

In addition to admonishing the majority for ignoring the obvious "object and purpose" of the Refugee Convention—which is to protect refugees or those who claim refugee status—Blackmun also derides his colleagues for ignoring the "ordinary meaning" of the term "return," noting that *Webster's Dictionary* defines the word as "to bring, send, or put (a person or thing) back to or in a former position." Like the majority, Blackmun believes that the inclusion of the French word "refouler" was meant to suggest that "return" means to "repulse" or to "drive back" or to "repel." However, in Blackmun's view, there is no apparent reason such acts of self-defense only apply to aliens literally at a country's borders or those who were already within the territory of that country. He makes his point by invoking famous war battles.

> Gage was repulsed (initially) at Bunker Hill. Lee was repelled at Gettysburg. Rommel was driven back across North Africa. The majority's puzzling progression ("refouler" means repel or drive back; therefore "return" means only exclude at a border; therefore the treaty does not apply) hardly justifies a departure from the path of ordinary meaning. The text of Article 33.1 is clear, and whether the operative term is "return" or "refouler," it prohibits the Government's actions. 509 U.S. at 192–193

As Blackmun points out, Article 33.1 does contain a geographical limitation. However, the only limitation is where a refugee cannot be sent *to*—states where the alien's life or freedom would be threatened—while there is absolutely no geographic restriction in terms of where aliens can be sent *from*. In his view, this is by no means surprising given the fact that the very aim of the Convention is to protect desperate individuals seeking safety.

Blackmun also addressed the majority's reliance on the remarks of the Swiss and Dutch delegates. He describes these remarks as "fragments" of the Convention's negotiating history, and he notes that these provisions were never voted on or adopted. Blackmun thereby concludes that rather than representing a "general consensus," as proclaimed by one of the delegates and as recognized as such by the U.S. Supreme Court, this position represented a decided minority opinion on the scope of the Convention's reach. In short, the Refugee Convention speaks for itself. Thus, there is no reason to give any kind of judicial deference to these statements.

Toward the end of the dissenting opinion, Blackmun sought to remind his colleagues, but the national and international community as well, of why the Refugee Convention was drafted in the first place. He writes,

> The Convention that the Refugee Act embodies was enacted largely in response to the experiences of Jewish refugees in Europe during the period of World War II. The tragic consequences of the world's indifference at that time are well known. The resulting ban on refoulement, as broad as the humanitarian purpose that inspired it, is easily applicable here, the Court's protestations or impotence and regret notwithstanding.

Justice Blackmun then concludes his dissent by charging the Court with perverting the very meaning of the Refugee Convention itself:

> The refugees attempting to escape from Haiti do not claim a right of admission to this country. They do not even argue that the Government has no right to intercept their boats. They demand only that the United States, land of refugees and guardian of freedom, cease forcibly driving them back to detention, abuse, and death. That is a modest plea, vindicated by the treaty and the statute. We should not close our ears to it.

As should be obvious, I believe that Justice Blackmun's interpretation of Article 33 of the Refugee Convention and Section 243 (h) (1) of the Immigration and Naturalization Act to be right and the majority of the Court wrong. As I mentioned earlier, the concept of human rights is not complicated, nor should it be made to be complicated. Although there is no "right" to be granted refugee protection in any country, there most certainly is a "right" not to be returned to a state where a person's life or freedom would be threatened. Thus, the entire purpose of the Refugee Convention is to assist and protect vulnerable people seeking to find human rights protection in a different land. The Court's approach does not do this. In fact, it goes far in achieving just the opposite end. What was left unsaid by the Court (perhaps for obvious reasons) is that there would be nothing "wrong" or "illegal" about having U.S. Coast Guard ships deliver refugees back to Haiti even if they were to face the prospect of certain death in their home country. In other words, what simply would not matter, at least according to the majority's approach, was how certain and how severe the persecution in Haiti would be for those "returned."

But why leave persecution and killing to Haitian agents? If the Refugee Convention does not have any extraterritorial application, as the Court maintains, there is no reason to believe that any other international human rights instrument would have an extraterritorial effect either. Under this concept of international human rights law, there would be nothing "wrong" or "illegal" with having U.S. Coast Guard personnel *themselves* carry out various human rights abuses against these hapless people. The same would also seem to be true of domestic law as well, particularly given the Court's slavish devotion to the presumption against the extraterritorial application of any domestic law even law that on its face deals with international events such as refugee protection. Of course, the Court would never announce that the law—or, more accurately, the absence of any law on the high seas—would (naturally) lead to this result. In other words, the Court would never say that there would be nothing unlawful (under either international or domestic law) that would prohibit U.S. Coast Guard personnel from killing or torturing individuals on the high seas themselves. However, this is exactly where the reasoning of the *Sale* decision takes us. And in my view, this is a perversion of both domestic and international law.

DENYING HUMAN RIGHTS PROTECTION OUTSIDE "EUROPE"

The second case we will look at is the European Court of Human Rights (ECHR) decision in *Bankovic v. Belgium* (2001). What has to be noted at the outset is that some of the harshest criticism of the U.S. Supreme Court decision in *Sale*—deserved criticism, in my view—came from European quarters. However, unwittingly or not, European states have essentially adopted this very same position regarding the scope of their own human rights obligations. In *Sale*, the Supreme Court held that nonrefoulement protection did not extend to individuals outside the United States. In *Bankovic*, the ECHR held that the human rights protections of the European Convention did not generally apply to individuals outside of "Europe." In both cases, territorial considerations were used as a way of demarcating, but really eliminating altogether, the protection of human rights (Roxstrom et al. 2005).

Bankovic arose from a NATO bombing mission over Belgrade in April 1999 that resulted in the deaths of sixteen civilians and injuries to that same number. The claimants/applicants brought suit against the group of NATO countries, which essentially consists of those states that are party to the European Convention plus the United States. In their complaint, they alleged that the European states were in violation of Article 2 (Right to Life), Article 10 (Freedom of Expression), and Article 13 (Right to an Effective Remedy) of the European Convention. However, the prior issue—and the sole question answered by the Court—was whether those individuals were within the "jurisdiction" of the European states for purposes of Article 1 of the European Convention, which reads, "The High Contracting Parties shall secure to everyone within their jurisdiction the rights and freedoms defined in . . . this Convention." The ECHR ruled that the claimants were not within the "jurisdiction" of the European states, and because of this the case was determined to be inadmissible.

One of the things that should be underscored is that the case concerned responsibility for something that the states had done as opposed to something that they had failed to do. The applicants' position is that the term "jurisdiction" in Article 1 is not referring to the territorial boundaries of these states but rather that the Contracting States must secure the rights and freedoms of the Convention to all those within or subject to their actual power. In other words, a Contracting State is bound by the Convention not only when it acts within its own territorial borders but also when it does so abroad. However, it is important to point out that the applicants' notion of "jurisdiction" is situation specific and that the Contracting States' obligations vis-à-vis individuals outside of their borders is commensurate with the extent of the actual authority or control over the human rights of these affected individuals. What this also means, then, is that for the purpose of determining Convention responsibility, the question whether or not a particular extraterritorial act was within the "jurisdiction" of the acting state(s) must be determined with reference to the specific facts and circumstances of that particular case.

The European states had a substantially different interpretation of the Convention. In their view, Article 1 had to be interpreted in accordance with its "ordinary meaning" in public international law. In their argument before the ECHR, they argued that the term "jurisdiction" in

Article 1 referred to the "assertion or exercise of legal authority, actual or purported, over persons owing some form of allegiance to that State or who have been brought within that State's control." Furthermore, the NATO states argued that jurisdiction "generally entails some form of structured relationship normally existing over a period of time." In their view, the European states had no previous relationship with any of the applicants, nor did these states ever assert any kind of legal authority over these persons. In short, those individuals who were killed or harmed were simply not within the "jurisdiction" of the Contracting States for purposes of Article 1.

The Court essentially adopted the respondent states' position. In its view, the European Convention was "essentially" or "primarily" territorial, although the Court had to admit (especially in light of some previous holdings) that the protections of the Convention could be extended beyond the territory of the European states when "exceptional circumstances" arose. The Court never sufficiently explained how or what constituted "exceptional circumstances." However, on the basis of the Court's decision in the *Bankovic* case, it must be concluded that dropping bombs on civilians does not constitute an "exceptional circumstance."

The most serious flaw in the Court's approach is that it essentially ignores the "object and purpose" of the European Convention itself, thereby violating the most basic principle of treaty interpretation (Orakhelashvili 2003). Like all other human rights instruments (including the Refugee Convention, I might add), the "object" of the Convention is human rights, while its "purpose" is the protection of those rights. Nothing could be simpler or more straightforward. It is this object and this purpose that should serve as the ultimate guide in interpreting the Convention. Thus, an interpretation of the Convention that fails to protect human rights should be seriously questioned if not immediately discarded. Yet, as I will show in a moment, this is exactly what the ECHR did in this case. Although the Court addressed a myriad of issues, I will focus on the following: the ECHR's questionable interpretation of the Convention's drafting history; its misrepresentation of the applicants' claim; the Court's questionable interpretation of state practice; and, finally, the Court's dangerous reading of other human rights treaties. We will then address the mess that *Bankovic* has made—not only for European domestic courts but also for itself.

Drafting History

As the Court was quick to point out, the earliest drafts of Article 1 limited the scope of the Convention to "all persons residing within their territories." However, this was subsequently changed to the current "within their jurisdiction" language. According to the Court, this did not change the "territorial" basis of the Convention, and it claimed to have "clear confirmation" for this from the following explanation provided by the drafting committee:

> The Assembly draft had extended the benefits of the Convention to "all persons residing within the territories of the signatory States." It seemed to the [drafting committee] that the term "residing" might be considered too restrictive. It was felt that the grounds for extending the benefits of the Convention to all persons in the territories of the signatory States, even those who could not be considered as residing in the legal sense of the world. The [drafting committee] therefore replaced the term "residing" by the words "within their jurisdiction" which are also contained in Article 2 of the Draft Convention of the United Nations Commission. (Council of Europe 1975)

There are at least two problems with what the ECHR has done. The first is that the Court is trying to reconcile two things that simply cannot be reconciled, namely, that the Convention can be both exclusively territorial but not exclusively territorial at the same time. In other words, the Court wants it both ways. It wants to say that the original draft used the term "territory" and that any subsequent changes were not intended to change this original intent. On the other hand, the Court acknowledges not only that the Convention has been applied extraterritorially but also that these extraterritorial readings are consonant with the drafters' intent. The point is that the Convention cannot be both exclusively territorial as well as extraterritorial at the same time. This, however, is exactly where the ECHR is attempting to position itself.

Leaving this quandary aside, the second problem is with the Court's reliance on the drafting history. While the language that is quoted by the Court might well lead to the territorial (or "essentially" or "primarily" territorial) conclusion that it draws, there is other language in the legislative history (but which is not quoted by the ECHR) that might well lead to an opposite conclusion. In particular, the drafters also went on to explain the rationale for the change in language by stating that the aim "is to *widen as far as possible* the categories of persons who are to benefit by the guarantee contained in the Convention" (emphasis supplied). While this passage, like the passage that was actually quoted by the ECHR, does not specifically address the issue of extraterritorial human rights violations, it does suggest that the drafters understood the benefits of the Convention were to be extended to human beings qua human beings, rather than on the basis of their membership in or level of attachment to the Contracting States.

The Treatment of the Applicants' Claim

One of the more unsettling aspects of the Court's opinion is the manner in which it sought to minimize the kinds of claims that it foresaw being brought if the applicants' position on the scope of Article 1 was to prevail. At one point it claimed that the applicants' position is "tantamount to arguing that anyone adversely affected by an act imputable to a Contracting State, wherever in the world that act may have been committed or its consequences felt, is thereby brought within the jurisdiction of that State for the purpose of Article 1 of the Convention" (par. 75).

To be sure, the applicants in *Bankovic* were more than "adversely affected" by the actions of the European states. Rather, sixteen people were killed and sixteen suffered injuries. Thus, the applicants were asserting the claim that they were victims of specific human rights violations prohibited by the Convention. This, of course, is vastly different than being "adversely affected." But in making this projection, the Court could then employ the specter that the entire European system of justice would be inundated by claims (and rather worthless claims at that) from "adversely affected" individuals from all corners of the globe.

Would there be an overload problem if the applicants' position had prevailed? This is quite possible, but this is also something that the European states themselves would have a great deal of control over. In other words, if these states did not violate human rights in countries outside of Europe there would be absolutely no reason to be concerned about this matter. However, after *Bankovic*, what we can be quite certain of is the opposite of this: non-Europeans who are victims of human rights abuses carried out by European states will have little (if any) means of enforcing or protecting those rights—either in Europe itself or anyplace else.

State Practice

Another rationale used by the Court was that the states themselves did not feel bound by the Convention in any of their activities outside their territorial borders. Or to state this another way, the Contracting States should not be bound by the Convention when acting extraterritorially because, at least to date, they have not felt as if they are bound. The Court explains its position:

> The Court finds State practice in the application of the Convention since its ratification to be indicative of a lack of any apprehension on the part of the Contracting States of their extra-territorial responsibilities in contexts similar to the present case. Although there have been a number of military missions involving Contracting States acting extra-territorially since their ratification of the Convention (inter alia, in the [Persian] Gulf, in Bosnia and Herzegovina and in the FRY), no State has indicated a belief that its extra-territorial actions involved an exercise of jurisdiction within the meaning of Article 1 of the Convention by making a derogation pursuant to Article 15 of the Convention. (par. 62)

There is a self-fulfilling prophecy at work here: according to the ECHR, states are not bound now because they have not felt bound in the past. There are, however, several strong arguments that can be made against this position. The first relates to Article 15 of the Convention, which does allow the Contracting States to derogate from certain provisions in the Convention during times of war. The Court's argument is that no state involved in these conflicts had invoked Article 15 in its military operations in other countries, which it then interpreted as meaning that these states felt as if the Convention simply did not apply to their operations in the first place. What this ignores is that derogations under Article 15 are restricted to times of war or a public emergency "threatening to the life of the nation." One would be extraordinarily hard pressed to say that any of the military activities the Court makes reference to would have been "threatening" to any of these countries in this same way. Thus, perhaps the Court is correct that no state had invoked Article 15 when acting outside its territorial borders because they were of the mind that the Convention itself did not apply. But another reason could be that these states felt (with good reason) that the "threatening to the life of the nation" standard could simply not be met in these various extraterritorial operations.

What also has to be said is that, while the Court used the lack of dero-gation as a way of supporting its position that the Convention did not ap-ply extraterritorially, one wonders how to handle the Falkland Islands war, which was never mentioned by the Court. You might recall that in the early 1980s there was a dispute between Argentina and Great Britain regarding ownership of this island, which resulted in a brief war in 1982 between these two states. What is noteworthy for present purposes is that Great Britain did not invoke Article 15 in this case either—in a war on the United Kingdom's "own" territory. Yet, surely, we would not conclude from this lack of derogation that the European Convention does not ap-ply on British "soil"! Why, then, should the ECHR automatically conclude that the Convention does not apply outside of "Europe" when states do not invoke Article 15 when they are acting outside their borders?

The final point relates to judicial abdication. States are quite capable of doing awful things. If we are to take from this that state behavior re-flects the status or even the existence of international law, then very lit-tle international human rights law would remain.

Comparison with Other International Human Rights Treaties

Another unfortunate move that the Court made was to compare the Eu-ropean Convention with several other international and regional hu-man rights treaties. The Court began this analysis by contrasting the "within their jurisdiction" language in the European Convention with common Article 1 of the Geneva Conventions, which reads, "The High Contracting Parties undertake to respect and to ensure respect for the present Convention *in all circumstances*" (emphasis supplied).

One thing that is wrong with this approach is that the Court does not even acknowledge that these two treaties were drafted by different peo-ple at a different time and for different purposes. Thus, differences in language should not be at all surprising. Beyond that, the ECHR never attempted to explore whether these differences had any real meaning— which they do not. All that this "in all circumstances" language was in-tended to accomplish was to underscore the non-reciprocal nature of the treaty itself. In short, there is no evidence that the ECHR was able to point to—or that it would be able to point to—in order to show that these differences in language in these two treaties was either purpose-ful or meaningful.

But what is even more dangerous is the Court's apparent (territorial) reading of virtually all other international treaties, especially the International Covenant on Civil and Political Rights (Political Covenant) and its 1966 Optional Protocol. Like the European Convention itself (or at least the Court's interpretation of it), the Court held that the language "within its territory and subject to its jurisdiction" in the Political Covenant and the "subject to its jurisdiction" language in Article 1 of the Optional Protocol was also generally territorial. Furthermore, the ECHR held that the extraterritorial jurisdiction recognized by the Human Rights Committee was of an "exceptional" nature but that it could not displace the plain meaning of the Political Covenant's textual limitation.

The Court commits a number of errors in its analysis. For one thing, the ECHR made note of the fact that early in the drafting process there were attempts to change the Political Covenant's "within its territory and subject to its jurisdiction" language but that this failure to change the language indicated that the treaty should be given a territorial reading. This is simply wrong. The reason the language was not changed is that several states (led by the United States) were concerned that their own citizens residing in other countries might attempt to hold them responsible for failure to carry out the provisions of the Political Covenant in this foreign land. Thus, the drafting history simply does not show what the ECHR claims it does. Nowhere is it suggested or implied in the drafting records that states should not be held responsible for their own acts based on the sole reason that these occurred outside of the Contracting State's territory. Rather, all that the drafting history shows is that states were anxious about behind held responsible for a failure to ensure the rights of the Covenant where the state in question lacked the legal competence to do so.

What is also disturbing is the manner in which the ECHR treats the Human Rights Committee's unanimous decision in *Lopez v. Uruguay*—a case that the Court does not even mention by name. In *Lopez*, the applicant claimed that her husband, a Uruguayan national, had been kidnapped in Argentina by members of the Uruguayan security force and had been secretly detained there before being brought back to Uruguay. The Uruguayan government denied these allegations but also held that the communication was inadmissible under the Optional Protocol because the Political Covenant did not apply to actions outside the territory of the state.

The Human Rights Committee soundly rejected Uruguay's position. It held that the language "individuals subject to its jurisdiction" in Article 1 of the Optional Protocol does not make reference "to the place where the violation occurred, but rather to the relationship between the individual and the State in relation to a violation of any of the rights set forth in the Covenant, wherever they occurred." The Committee went on to hold that Article 2 (1) of the Political Covenant, which refers to both "territory" and "jurisdiction," simply imposes a mandate of the Contracting States to uphold the Covenant within their national territories but that it says nothing that would permit states to perpetrate Covenant violations in the territory of another state. Finally, to underscore its support for the extraterritorial application of the Political Covenant, the Committee expressed the view that "it would be unconscionable to so interpret the responsibility under article 2 of the Covenant to permit a State party to perpetrate violations of the Covenant on the territory of another State, which violations it could not perpetrate on its own territory" (par. 12.3).

I will close this discussion by making two points. The first relates to the Court's treatment of the *Lopez* decision itself. Even assuming that the absence of a citation to *Lopez* was purely accidental, what the Court did in summarily dismissing the case was to show a complete and utter disregard for the work done by the international body that is authorized to interpret the Political Covenant. The second point is that what might be even more disturbing is that the Court apparently is of the belief that all (or virtually all) international human rights laws do not bind a state when it operates outside its borders. Of course, the Court is not saying that states should be able to torture, commit summary executions, discriminate on the basis of race and gender, and so on—so long as this is done outside the state's borders. However, the problem is that, given the Court's approach to the issue, there is simply no law that would prevent states from doing these very things.

The *Bankovic* Mess

You will recall that the Court is not taking the position that the European Convention never applies outside of "Europe," only that there must be "exceptional circumstances" for this to happen. So what constitutes an "exceptional circumstance"? One of the reasons *Bankovic* is such a baffling and frustrating case is that prior to this decision the rule that had been established was that the Convention *did* apply outside of Europe when European countries were operating in this realm. This is most clearly seen in the situation involving Turkey's occupation of northern Cyprus where in a series of decisions both the European Commission on Human Rights and the European Court of Human Rights had held that the Convention applied to Turkish operations. One of the best examples of this is *Cyprus v. Turkey* (1975), where the European Commission on Human Rights unanimously held that

> In Art. 1 of the Convention, the High Contracting Parties undertake to secure the rights and freedoms . . . to everyone "within their jurisdiction . . . ." The Commission finds that this term is not . . . equivalent to or limited to the national territory of the High Contracting Party concerned. It is clear from this language . . . and the object of this Article, and from the purpose of the Convention as a whole, that the High Contracting Parties are bound to secure the said rights and freedoms to all persons under their actual authority and responsibility, whether that authority is exercised within their own territory or abroad. (Par. 8)

What the *Bankovic* court attempted to do was to substantially limit these previous holdings. In that way, the Court conceded that the Convention would be applicable to an effective military occupation of another Contracting State. However, the ECHR presented the argument (or at least the conclusion) that this situation was qualitatively different than the situation involved in *Bankovic*. Why dropping bombs and killing and/or injuring people is not also a form of exercising "effective control" is highly debatable (Lawson 2004). However, it is some of the Court's subsequent rulings that are perhaps even more difficult to understand.

The first case is *Ocalan v. Turkey* (2000), which is based on an extraterritorial arrest (in Kenya) of the Kurdish revolutionary leader (Ocalan). As in *Bankovic*, the central question was whether the Convention applied or not. Was Ocalan within the "jurisdiction" of one of the Contracting States (Turkey) when he was arrested at the Nairobi airport? The Court held that Ocalan was within Turkey's jurisdiction and, thus, Ocalan would be able to receive European Convention protection: "The Court considers the circumstances of the present case are distinguishable from those in the aforementioned Bankovic and Others case, notably in that the applicant was physically forced to return to Turkey by Turkish authorities and was subject to their authority and control following his arrest and return to Turkey" (par. 93).

How is *Ocalan* to be interpreted? Recall that the ECHR has stated that the European Convention is "primarily" or "essentially" territorial but that it could be applied to extraterritorial actions under "exceptional circumstances." *Ocalan* seems to be creating a new "exceptional circumstances" category—for extraterritorial arrests. Thus, the Court seems to be recognizing two completely different situations when the Convention applies to actions outside of Europe. One is the military occupation of another country—or at least the military occupation of another Contracting State; that much remains unclear. On the other extreme is a simple arrest carried out in a foreign land. In between, one might well imagine, there are an enormous number of situations where European states "act" outside of "Europe." But what remains unclear is when (if ever) these other actions rise to the level of an "exceptional circumstance" so that those who are acted upon have some protection under the European Convention.

Consider *United Kingdom v. Al-Skeini* (2004), a domestic (U.K.) case involving six killings carried out by British troops operating in Iraq. The question is a familiar one: does the European Convention apply to actions taken by European states outside of "Europe"? Were these civilians within the "jurisdiction" of the United Kingdom at the time they were killed by British forces?

There are several ways the Court could have approached this problem, given the ECHR's *Bankovic* precedent. On the one hand, since British troops are physically on the ground in Iraq (unlike the situation in *Bankovic*), the Court might have concluded that the entirety of Iraq was within the "jurisdiction" of the United Kingdom and that Great Britain was bound by the Convention in its operations throughout the country. Another approach might have been to limit the reach of the Convention to the southern region of Iraq, where British troops have been concentrated, or perhaps to particular cities or towns (i.e., Basra) that have been under British authority and control. However, what the British High Court held was that the European Convention only applied to the one killing that had occurred in a British prison—but not to any of the deaths that took place on the streets of Baghdad. If there is some logic to this distinction I am not aware of it. Apparently, a state exercises jurisdiction over a person when it arrests him and it detains him, but not necessarily when it exercises the "ultimate jurisdiction"—by killing him (Altiparmak 2004).

It is not only domestic courts in Europe that will have to deal with the meaning of *Bankovic*. Rather, the Court itself has had to struggle with its own creation. In *Ilascu and Others v. Moldova and Russia* (2004), the Court was dealing with the opposite situation of *Bankovic*. In this case, the applicants were attempting to hold Moldova responsible for human rights violations that occurred within the physical territory of Moldova but that was under the "jurisdiction" of the former Soviet Union (the new Russian Republic). For the Court, Moldova's inability to control this part of its territory simply did not matter, and in a mechanical (and territorial) fashion it held Moldova responsible for human rights violations that it was not able to prevent.

What are the implications of this holding? For one thing, it would seem to suggest that European countries that have housed secret CIA detention facilities would be "responsible" under the Convention for human rights violations that were carried out by American CIA officials. The reason for this, to use the Court's own logic, is that these events occurred within the "territory" of these respective states and, thus, were within each state's "jurisdiction." Furthermore, there is the case involving Hassan Mustafa Osama Nasr, who was abducted by CIA operatives on a Milan street in 2003 and sent to Egypt where he was subjected to torture. According to the *Ilascu* ruling, because the abduction had taken place within Italy's territorial borders, the Italian government would be "responsible" for these human rights violations— whether or not Italian authorities were operating in tandem with the CIA or not.

A second case is *Issa v. Turkey* (2000), and it is based on a claim brought by a group of Iraqis who claimed that Turkish officials, operating on Iraqi territory, had violated various provisions of the European Convention. One thing that is interesting to note is that the Turkish government had not originally contested the fact that the applicants would have been within their "jurisdiction"; however, it did so following the ECHR's ruling in *Bankovic*.

In addressing this claim, the Court began with what it now considers to be the correct interpretation of Article 1. It described *Bankovic* as the "established case law in this area," and the Court employed the same language that the Convention was "primarily" territorial. Yet, the Court seemed to make some effort to soften *Bankovic* by then stating that "the acts of Contracting States performed outside their territory or which produce effects there may amount to exercise by them of their jurisdiction." Turning to the applicants' claim that Turkish officials had deliberately tortured, killed, and mutilated their relatives, the Court held that it "does not exclude the possibility that, as a consequence of [Turkey's military actions in Iraq], the respondent State could be considered to have exercised, temporarily, effective overall control of a particular portion of the territory of northern Iraq" (par. 77).

Yet, after announcing what appeared to be yet another "exceptional circumstance" that would invoke the European Convention in an extraterritorial fashion—the "temporary effective overall control over a particular portion of the territory of a non-European state" standard, if you will—the Court then beat a hasty retreat and held, in a puzzling fashion, that there was no evidence that Turkish troops had actually ever entered Iraqi territory, and it thereby dismissed the case.

The problem is that the Court is wedded to an effective control standard that simply misreads the nature of human rights. It is impossible to imagine more heinous human rights violations than the deliberate torture, mutilation, and killing of innocent civilians—which is exactly what the applicants in *Issa* were claiming. Still, under the ECHR's approach, it would not have been sufficient if the applicants had established that Turkey had carried out these acts. Rather, the applicants would also have to prove to the Court that Turkey had exercised some degree of effective control—temporary or otherwise—over the particular piece of land where these violations were said to have occurred. Consider an alternative scenario. Suppose that, rather than entering Iraqi territory, Turkish officials had simply shot across the border and in so doing had killed a group of Iraqi civilians. Under the Court's holding in *Bankovic* and *Issa*, Turkey would not have exercised "jurisdiction" over these now-dead civilians. The absurdity of this position should be apparent.

The only important issue should be whether a violation of human rights had taken place and who was responsible for directing or carrying out this violation. What did not matter—or at least, what should not matter—is whether Turkish troops had actually entered Iraqi territory or not. All that should have mattered in any of these cases was that, as a Contracting State, Turkey has an obligation under the European Convention not to kill, mutilate, torture, and harm—no matter where this occurs and no matter who the victims of these actions would happen to be.

The problem with *Bankovic* and the cases that follow is that the decision stands for the proposition that human rights are not owed to people because they are human beings but because they live (and die) in a particular place and/or by particular means. The damage done by this case will not be undone by simply creating additional categories of "exceptional circumstances." Instead, the damage can only be undone by recognizing that European states should be held responsible for *all* of the human rights violations that they carry out, no matter where this occurs.

THE AMERICAN "WAR ON TERROR"

Territorial considerations have also played a central role in the manner in which the U.S. government has conducted its so-called war on terror. The most obvious manifestation of this has been that almost every one of the so-called enemy combatants has been held in detention facilities outside the United States, most notably, at the U.S. military base at Guantanamo Bay, Cuba, rather than on American soil itself. According to the position of the Bush administration, neither domestic (U.S.) law nor American obligations under international law apply to this base, or to any other foreign detention facility where "enemy combatants" are being held.

Interestingly enough, this territorial argument has not been accepted (fully) by the U.S. Supreme Court. This issue was most squarely presented in *Rasul v. Bush* (2004). The petitioners in this case were two Australian citizens and twelve Kuwaiti nationals who were challenging their detention as "enemy combatants" under the federal (U.S.) habeas statute, which grants federal district courts to hear habeas petitions "within their respective jurisdictions." The position of the U.S. government was that these detainees were not within the "jurisdiction" of the United States and, thus, that the case should be dismissed.

The leading case in support of the government's position was *Johnson v. Eisentrager* (1950), where the Supreme Court had denied a petition for relief filed by a group of twenty-one German citizens who had been captured by U.S. forces in China, tried, and convicted of war crimes by an American military commission headquartered in Nanking, and then incarcerated in the Landsberg Prison in occupied Germany. The Court of Appeals had found jurisdiction in this matter on the grounds that "any person who is deprived of his liberty by officials of the United States, acting under purported authority of that Government, and who can show that his confinement is in violation of a prohibition of the Constitution, has a right to the writ." However, in *Eisentrager*, the U.S. Supreme Court overturned this decision, reasoning as follows:

> We are here confronted with a decision whose basic premise is that these prisoners are entitled, as a constitutional right, to sue in some court of the United States for a writ of habeas corpus. To support that assumption we must hold that a prisoner of our military authorities is constitutionally entitled to the writ, even though he a) is an enemy alien; b) has never been or resided in the United States; c) was captured outside of our territory and there held in military custody as a prisoner of war; d) was tried and convicted by a Military Commission sitting outside the United States; e) for offenses against laws of war committed outside the United States; f) and is at all times imprisoned outside the United States. 339 U.S. at 777.

For the *Rasul* court, *Eisentrager* differed from the case before it in every one of these ways:

> Petitioners . . . differ from the *Eisentrager* detainees in important respects: They are not nationals of countries at war with the United States, and they deny that they have engaged in or plotted acts of aggression against the United States; they have never been afforded access to any tribunal, much less charged with and convicted of wrongdoing; and for more than two years they have been imprisoned in territory over which the United States exercises exclusive jurisdiction and control. 542 U.S. at 476.

One of the central issues in *Rasul* involved the status of Guantanamo Bay, Cuba, itself. As the majority points out, under the terms of the 1903 Lease Agreement, the United States exercises "complete jurisdiction and control" over the base, and it may continue to exercise such control permanently, if it so chooses. Moreover, the government itself conceded that the habeas statute would create federal court jurisdiction over the claims of an American citizen held at the base. The Court then concluded from this that the habeas statute draws no distinction between Americans and aliens held in federal custody and concluded that there was "little reason to think that Congress intended the geographic coverage of the statute to vary depending on the detainee's citizenship." 542 U.S. at 481.

Justice Kennedy's concurring opinion pushed the unique nature of Guantanamo Bay even further stating that "what matters is the unchallenged and indefinite control that the United States has long exercised over Guantanamo Bay." Kennedy continues, "From a practical perspective, the indefinite lease of Guantanamo Bay has produced a place that belongs to the United State, extending the 'implied protection' of the United States to it" (citing *Eisentrager*). 542 U.S. at 487.

In his dissenting opinion, Justice Scalia claims that the majority has extended the federal habeas statute to the "four corners of the earth." However, it is by no means clear that this is what the Court has done—or that this is what it intended to do. Rather, in many ways *Rasul* could be read as a Guantanamo Bay–only decision in the sense that there is no other military facility outside the territorial borders of the United States where the U.S. government exercises anywhere near the kind of "sovereignty" or "jurisdiction" than it does over this one, particular base.

What has ensued since this time is a continuing struggle between the political branches and the Supreme Court. In response to *Rasul*, Congress passed the Detainee Treatment Act of 2005, which sought to limit judicial review of claims brought by "enemy combatants." In *Hamdan v. Rumsfeld* (2006), the Court held that this act was not intended to apply to habeas claims that had already been filed. In turn, in 2006, Congress signed into law the Military Commissions Act, which sought to address this matter. What remains unclear is how the Court (as well as the new Congress) will respond to this. The point is that even if the habeas option remains, it is still not clear that it would apply to any U.S. military detention facility other than Guantanamo Bay, Cuba.

Territorial considerations—and "state responsibility" considerations—are also behind the U.S. practice of "extraordinary renditions" (Center for Human Rights and Global Justice 2004). Under this policy, suspected "terrorists" under American custody are turned over to "sympathetic" governments, which in turn then carry out torture in order to obtain information for the United States. One of the best known cases of an "extraordinary rendition" involved Maher Arar, who is a dual national of Canada and Syria. On his way back to his home in Canada in

September 2002, Arar was detained and interrogated at a New York airport following a stopover. He was then interrogated and detained there for several days before he was delivered to Syrian authorities, where Arar was subjected to torture over the course of several months before he was eventually released and allowed to return to Canada. After an extensive inquiry, the Canadian government has exonerated Arar of having any ties with international terrorism and awarded him nearly ten million dollars in damages.

The question is whether the United States is in violation of international law. Arar is a fairly easy and straightforward case because Arar had been on American soil and then flown to Syria. In this case, the United States would be in violation of the nonrefoulement provision (Article 3) of the Torture Convention, which reads, "No State Party shall expel, return ("refouler") or extradite a person to another State where there are substantial grounds for believing that he would be in danger of being subjected to torture."

But it is important to note that what differentiates the Arar case from most other cases of "extraordinary rendition" is that Arar was sent out from the United States. The overwhelming majority of those subject to this procedure by American officials are transferred from some other locale in the world (but not the United States). The point is that these other individuals have never been within the "territory" of the United States. And if the Torture Convention is without extraterritorial effect—as the European Court of Human Rights (among others) has suggested—then there might be nothing unlawful about "extraordinary renditions."

Most people will have no trouble seeing behind this façade. My sense is that most will clearly recognize that the U.S. government is behind these acts of torture—no matter where they take place and no matter who carries out this torture—and they would see the United States as being "responsible" for these acts of torture. However, my point is that "extraordinary renditions" represent an extreme situation where territorial demarcations are being used as a means of avoiding state responsibility for violations of human rights.

CONCLUSION

What we have examined in this chapter is the way in which Western states have operated under the belief that they have one set of human rights obligations at home—but a different set of obligations (but really no obligations at all) when they are operating outside their territorial boundaries. Perhaps even more important, states have created this distinction not only in terms of positive obligations (which we will turn to in the next chapter) but also in terms of the negative obligation not to cause harm. To be clear, Western states do not claim that they have a "right" to harm people outside their own borders, and certainly no court will proclaim or recognize this right either. However, what these states have argued—and what some of the leading judicial bodies in the world have given license to—is an interpretation of international and domestic law that allows for such a distinction. In the *Sale* decision, the U.S. Supreme Court held that American obligations not to return a person to a place where her life or freedom would be threatened only arose if and when this person was either right at the borders of the United States or already inside this country, but not before then. This means that individuals on the high seas have no protection against the actions of American agents. European actors sharply criticized this decision, but in *Bankovic* the European Court of Human Rights essentially gave the same territorial understanding to human rights. In this case, the Court held that foreign nationals outside of "Europe" who were harmed by the actions of European states were outside the "jurisdiction" of the Contracting States and, thus, were outside the scope of the Convention's protections.

Finally, we took a brief look at the role that territory has played in the American "war on terror." No doubt, the starkest manifestation of this thinking that human rights protections are based on territorial considerations can be found in the U.S. policy of "extraordinary rendition," whereby suspected "terrorists" are turned over to a foreign country for "interrogation" purposes. According to the Bush administration, these "extraordinary renditions" do not implicate the United States (even when done under the direction of American officials and even when "intelligence" thereby gathered is relied upon by U.S. officials). The rationale is that this torture is carried out in other lands and by agents of another country.

Yet, I believe that very few people buy into this for the simple reason that it is quite obvious that the U.S. government is most decidedly the moving force "behind" the torture—no matter where the torture takes place and no matter who actually carries it out. But "extraordinary renditions" represent the easy case. What is much more difficult to decipher are the myriad of other ways where Western states continue to use "territory" as a means of escaping any responsibility for the human rights violations that they carry out in foreign lands.

REFERENCES

Altiparmak, Kerem. 2004. "*Bankovic*: An Obstacle to the Application of the European Convention on Human Rights in Iraq?" *Journal of Conflict and Security Law* 9:213–51.

Bankovic et al. v. Belgium et al. App. No. 52207/99 Eur. Ct. H.R. (2001) 41 I.L.M 517.

Center for Human Rights and Global Justice. 2004. *Torture by Proxy: International Law and Domestic Law Applicable to "Extraordinary Renditions."* The Committee on International Human Rights of the Association of the Bar of the City of New York and the Center for Human Rights and Global Justice, New York University.

Council of Europe (Directorate of Human Rights). 1975. *Collected Edition of the "Travaux Preparatoires" of the European Convention on Human Rights.* Vol. III.

Cyprus v. Turkey. App. Nos. 6780/74, 6950/75, 2 Eur. Comm'n H.R. Dec. & Rep. (1975).

Detainee Treatment Act of 2005. Pub. L. 109-148, 119 Stat. 2739.

Federal (U.S.) Habeas Corpus Statute. 28 U.S.C. Sec. 2241 (a).

Hamdan v. Rumsfeld. 126 S. Ct. 2749 (2006).

Ilascu v. Russia and Moldova. App. No. 48787/99, Eur. Ct. H.R. July 8, 2004 Roxtrom, Erik, Mark Gibney and Terje Einarsen. 2005. "The NATO Bombing Casee and the Limits of Western Human Rights Protection." *Boston University International Law Journal* 23:55–136.

Issa v. Turkey. App. No. 31821/96, Eur. Ct. H.R. (2000) (Dec. on admis.).

Johnson v. Eisentrager. 339 U.S. 763 (1950).

Lawson, Rick. 2004. "Life after Bankovic: On the Extraterritorial Application of the European Convention on Human Rights," in Fons Coomans and Menno T. Kamminga (eds.), *Extraterritorial Application of Human Rights Treaties.* Antwerp, Belgium: Intersentia.

Lopez Burgos v. Uruguay. Communication No. R.12/52 (6 June 1979) U.N. Doc. Supp. No. 40 (A/36/40).

Military Commissions Act of 2006. Pub. L. No. 109-366, 120 Stat. 2600.

Ocalan v. Turkey. App. No. 46221/99, Eur. Ct. H.R. (2000) (Dec. on admis.).

Orakhelashvili, Alexander. 2003. "Restrictive Interpretation of Human Rights Treaties in the Recent Jurisprudence of the European Court of Human Rights." *European Journal of International Law* 14:529–68.

Rasul v. Bush. 546 U.S. 466 (2004).

4

STEP THREE: ACCOUNTABILITY

S tates have not taken human rights seriously. This is true, most obviously, of countries that torture and kill people and systematically deny various other human rights, but to a large extent this can be said of *all* states.

Human rights have become something that it should never have become and the opposite of what its framers intended it to be. Human rights are now commonly thought of as being "aspirational" or "inspirational"—or even worse, perhaps, simply "nice." The problem is that human rights should be anything but "nice." As Johannes Morsink emphasizes throughout his seminal book on the drafting history of the Universal Declaration of Human Rights (UDHR), what the framers of that document wanted above all else was to create an "aggressive" human rights (Morsink 1999). What we have instead is the very opposite of aggressiveness the data simply lead to no other conclusion. Given the levels of starvation, killings, illiteracy, torture, and so on, I think it would be fair to say that the framers would be appalled and outraged at the manner in which states treat their own citizens. Yet, what they would also find appalling and outrageous is the way in which all other states—and not simply those that commit cruelties against their own citizens—have failed to meet their obligations under international human rights law.

International human rights law creates certain domestic responsibilities for member states, but it also creates certain international or extraterritorial responsibilities as well. When countries become a state party to these various international human rights treaties, they legally obligate themselves to carry out both sets of obligations. As Sigrun Sko-gly has pointed out, extraterritorial obligations are not about introduc-ing "new" human rights obligations but rather about simply recognizing and honoring and protecting human rights obligations that already ex-ist and that are spelled out rather clearly in various international hu-man rights treaties. The third step, then, is really quite elementary. States should meet all of their obligations under international law—and they should be held accountable for their failure to do so.

UNITED NATIONS CHARTER

Since so much of our present-day "human rights revolution" is a reac-tion to the horrors of World War II, perhaps the place to begin is with the establishment of the United Nations, which was viewed (correctly) as one of the key instruments in creating the desired new world order. The Preamble of the U.N. Charter is divided into three sections, only two of which will concern us. The first section makes reference to the horrors of the recent past. However, like the organization that was be-ing created, the focus is decidedly on the future. Thus, the Charter be-gins with states declaring their motives and their intentions in creating this new international institution:

> to save succeeding generations from the scourge of war, which twice in our lifetime has brought untold sorrow to mankind, and
> to reaffirm faith in fundamental human rights, in the dignity and worth of the human person, in the equal rights of men and women and of nations large and small, and
> to establish conditions under which justice and respect for the oblig-ations arising from treaties and other sources of international law can be maintained, and to promote social progress and better standards of life in larger freedom.

The second section of the Preamble then sets forth the ends of this new United Nations:

> to practice tolerance and live together in peace with one another as good neighbors, and

> to unite our strength to maintain international peace and security, and to ensure, by the acceptance of principles and the institution of methods, that armed force shall not be used, save in the common interest, and
>
> to employ international machinery for the promotion of the economic and social advancement of all peoples.

There are two things that must be said about the Preamble in particular and the United Nations in general. The first is that the ultimate goal is to minimize, and perhaps even eliminate, human suffering—from war, certainly, but from other causes as well. The second is the explicit recognition that the only way of achieving this end is through international efforts, specifically recognized in the Preamble's promise to "employ *international machinery* for the promotion of the economic and social advances of all peoples" (emphasis supplied). This point is made even clearer in Article 1, which lists as one of the purposes of the United Nations "to achieve *international cooperation* in solving *international problems* of an economic, social, cultural, or humanitarian character" (emphases supplied).

Further on in Article 56, the Charter demands that "all Members pledge themselves to take *joint and separate action*, in cooperation with the Organization for the achievement of the purposes set forth in Article 55" (emphasis supplied). And what are these purposes set forth in Article 55?

1. higher standards of living, full employment, and conditions of economic and social progress and development;
2. solutions to international economic, social, health, and related problems; and international cultural and educational cooperation; and
3. universal respect for, and observance of, human rights and fundamental freedoms for all without distinction as to race, sex, language, or religion.

The point is that the United Nations Charter is quite clear and very specific about states' extraterritorial duties, especially in the realm of economic deprivation. States pledge to work with the organization, but they also pledge to work with one another—and to do so in order to achieve certain ends. This pledge, it needs to be said, is not an ethical or moral pledge; rather, it is a legal pledge.

THE INTERNATIONAL BILL OF RIGHTS

The International Bill of Rights is a term commonly used to describe the troika consisting of the Universal Declaration of Human Rights and the Economic and Political Covenants. Of these, only the two Covenants have status as being "law," although a very strong argument could be made that the UDHR has also become binding on all states through customary international law.

However, this discussion of what is or what is not binding law has a surreal quality to it because there is not a single aspect of international human rights law that truly has been "binding" on states as such. Rather, international human rights law has been neutered, better treated as a theoretical concept or even a hypothetical idea or ideal. Is this what the framers intended to accomplish? The brief answer is no. The drafters were men and women who had witnessed massive levels of human suffering. The whole point of their efforts—the reason the United Nations was created; the reason the Universal Declaration was drafted; the reason international human rights law has come into existence—was to avoid these horrors, this nightmare, once and for all. As Morsink describes it, those responsible for drafting the UDHR had a "strong desire to see to it that human rights talk was not just talk, but coupled with the necessary machinery of implementation and realization" (Morsink 1999: 12).

Universal Declaration of Human Rights

It is well known that the UDHR combines together what are now commonly referred to as two sets of rights: civil and political rights, on the one hand, and economic, social, and cultural rights. For those drafting the document, however, there was no hierarchy of rights. Thus, there was none of the present-day thinking that political and civil rights are "real" but that economic, social, and cultural rights are something other than "rights." This, however, is not to say that the two sets of rights did not differ from one another. As Morsink notes, the drafters were well aware that civil and political rights were more common—certainly in the various constitutions of the constituent states—and, thus, more commonly accepted. What economic, social, and cultural rights represented, then, were more challenging cases—more challenging because their implementation was to be based on unprecedented levels of international assistance and cooperation.

The UDHR not only applies to every human right, but also its provisions protect every human being. In the stirring language of the Preamble,

> The General Assembly Proclaims this Universal Declaration of Human Rights as a common standard of achievement for all peoples and all nations to the end that every individual and every organ of society, keeping this Declaration constantly in mind, shall strive by teaching and education to promote respect for these rights and freedoms and by progressive measures, *national and international,* to secure their universal and effective recognition and observance, both among the peoples of Member States themselves and among the peoples of territories under their jurisdiction. (emphasis supplied)

Beyond this, there is scarcely a provision in the document that does not attest to the idea that these declared human rights were to be enjoyed by "all" or by "everyone" and that "no one" was to be denied human rights protection.

Yet, not only are "rights" universal but so are the obligations to meet those rights. This is most clearly spelled out in Articles 22 and 28. Article 22 reads,

> Everyone, as a member of society, has the right to social security and is entitled to realization, *through national effort and international cooperation and in accordance with the organization and resources of each State,* of the economic, social and cultural rights indispensable for his dignity and the free development of his personality. (emphasis supplied)

Article 28 does not deal with any particular right. Rather, its concern is with the kind of world order that would have to be created in order to best protect the human rights set forth in the Universal Declaration itself. Article 28 reads, "Everyone is entitled to a *social and international order* in which the rights and freedoms set forth in this Declaration are fully realized" (emphasis supplied).

The question is this: to what extent have states engaged in the kind of international cooperation required of them in Article 22? And how often have states (or, for that matter, *any* state) been concerned with the "social and international order" necessary to protect human rights as demanded by Article 28?

The other two legs of the International Bill of Rights—the International Covenant on Civil and Political Rights (Political Covenant) and the International Covenant on Economic, Social and Cultural Rights (Economic Covenant)—represent the unfortunate demarcation of human rights into two distinct and separate classes. Of the two, the International Covenant on Civil and Political Rights is generally seen as protecting "negative" rights while the International Covenant on Economic, Social and Cultural Rights is typically viewed as protecting "positive" rights. However, what is ironic is that states' extraterritorial obligations are spelled out much clearer in the Economic Covenant than in the Political Covenant. The cruel thing, of course, is that in both instances extraterritorial obligations have in large part been ignored.

International Covenant on Economic, Social and Cultural Rights

One of the first things to note about the Economic Covenant is the *absence* of certain language—the terms "jurisdiction" and "territory" in particular—that appears in many other international human rights treaties. A case in point is the Political Covenant whose scope is set forth in Article 2 (1): "Each State Party to the present Covenant undertakes to respect and ensure to all individuals *within its territory and subject to its jurisdiction* the rights recognized in the present Covenant" (emphasis supplied). As we will see later, some have interpreted this language to mean that the provisions of the Political Convention only apply within each member state's territorial boundaries—but that a state is thereby free to ignore this law when it operates outside its own borders.

I do not want to get too far into this argument, at least at this point, because the more important thing to note is that the International Covenant on Economic, Social and Cultural Rights does *not* have this same kind of restrictive language. Rather, Article 2 (1) of the Economic Covenant reads,

Each State Party to the present Covenant undertakes to take steps, *individually and through international assistance and cooperation*, especially economic and technical, to the maximum of its available resources, with a view to achieving progressively the full realization of the rights recognized in the present Covenant by all appropriate means, including particularly the adoption of legislative measures. (emphasis supplied)

The extraterritorial nature of the Economic Covenant is also spelled out in Article 11. Paragraph 1 provides,

The State Parties to the present Covenant recognize the right of everyone to an adequate standard of living for himself and his family, including adequate food, clothing and housing, and to the continuous improvement of living conditions. The State Parties will take appropriate steps to ensure the realization of this right, recognizing to this effect the *essential importance of international cooperation* based on free consent. (emphasis supplied)

Paragraph 2 reads,

The States Parties to the present Convention, recognizing the fundamental right of everyone to be free from hunger, shall take, *individually and through international cooperation*, the measures, including specific programs, which are needed:

a) To improve methods of production, conservation and distribution of food by making full use of the principles of nutrition and by developing or reforming agrarian systems in such a way as to achieve the most efficient development and utilization of natural resources.
b) Taking into account the problems of both food-importing and food-exporting countries, to *ensure an equitable distribution of world food supplies* in relation to need. (emphases supplied)

Although states look askance at the prospect of having any legal obligations to assist individuals in other states whose rights under the Covenant are being violated, this should be anything but the case. States' extraterritorial obligations are set forth quite clearly. What part of "international assistance and cooperation," or "international cooperation," is so difficult to understand? Moreover, from her definitive study of this issue, Sigrun Skogly has concluded that there was a "general consensus" among the drafters of the International Covenant on

Economic, Social and Cultural Rights that the rights set forth in the document would have to be protected through international means. She writes,

> The drafting history of Article 2 (1) shows that there are some inconsistencies in the approaches held as to the concrete meaning of *through international co-operation and assistance*. However, it seems that the delegations were quite agreed that international co-operation and assistance is needed for the full implementation of the rights, and that the resources available based upon this co-operation and assistance should be part of the resources used for the full realization of these rights. (Skogly 2006: 86, emphasis in original)

It is often said that the International Covenant on Economic, Social and Cultural Rights is "different" from all other human rights instruments in the sense that the law itself does not demand immediate implementation. Rather, it is argued (based on the language in Article 2 [1], quoted above) that the Covenant only calls for the "progressive realization" of these rights, based on a state committing its "maximum available resources" to achieve this result. What this also means is that if a state has few "available resources," "progressive realization" of these rights will be slow in coming—which is a nice way of saying that, for a country like Tanzania, there might not be anything "unlawful" even when several million people starve to death.

The Covenant's language means what it says. However, it does not mean what Western states think it means. Consider the notion of "maximum available resources." The standard interpretation is to limit this to each state's own resources—but only that state's resources. The fatal flaw in this approach is that many other countries' excess resources are also "available," and the first state should also be able to factor these in as well. Furthermore, if the Covenant's provisions demanding "international assistance and cooperation" mean what they say—and my point is that they most certainly do—these resources *must* be considered when determining "available resources."

To be clear, then, there are two ways of computing "maximum available resources." One is to look solely at the resources that a particular state has, and nothing beyond this. The other way is to *begin* by looking at a state's own resources—but to then look to the "available resources" of other states as well. It would be safe to say that, for poor states, the amount "available" in the first instance will be substantially less than it would be when rich states have met their legal obligation to provide "international assistance and cooperation." What this also means is that we should be far less sanguine about the notion of "progressive realization" than we have been. This term has repeatedly been used to defend what would otherwise be thought of as outrageous human rights violations, the rationale being that because of a state's lack of "available resources," "progressive realization" meant that economic rights were simply not going to be protected for quite a period of time and for quite a number (literally billions) of people.

Unfortunately, states have universally and systematically ignored this second reading. However, there are indications that this approach will no longer go unchallenged—even if state practice remains unchanged because of the lack of any effective remedy. The most noteworthy development is that the Committee on Economic, Social and Cultural Rights, the United Nations committee responsible for implementing and interpreting the Economic Covenant, has started to provide some real meaning to the term "international assistance and cooperation," and along with this, the Committee has begun to press states on their efforts at meeting their extraterritorial obligations.

In one of its earliest General Comments (No. 3, 1990), the Committee described the term "maximum available resources" as referring to "both the resources existing within a State and those available from the international community through international cooperation and assistance" (par. 13). The Committee then proceeded to push this argument even further:

> It is particularly incumbent upon those states that are in a position to assist others in this regard. . . . It [the Committee] emphasizes that, in the absence of an active programme of international assistance and cooperation on the part of all those States that are in a position to undertake one, the full realization of economic, social and cultural rights will remain an unfulfilled aspiration in many countries. (par. 14)

In General Comment Number 12 on the Right to Food (1999), the Committee asserted that state parties have an obligation to "take steps to respect the enjoyment of the right to food in other countries, to protect that right, to facilitate access to food and to provide the necessary aid when required" (par. 12). Furthermore, the Committee has continued to explain and promote the meaning of "international assistance and co-operation" in other General Comments. Most notably, in its General Comment on the Right to Health (No. 14, 2000), the Committee stated that, "depending on the availability of resources, States should facilitate access to essential health facilities, goods and services in other countries, wherever possible and provide the necessary aid when required" (par. 39). Furthermore, in its General Comment on the Right to Water (No. 15, 2002), the Committee stated that "international assistance should be provided in a manner that is consistent with the Covenant and other human rights standards and sustainable and culturally appropriate. The economically developed States parties have a special responsibility and interest to assist the poorer developing States in this regard" (par. 34).

As Skogly has pointed out, one of the Committee's most noteworthy contributions regarding the scope of the Covenant was General Comment Number 8 (1997) dealing with economic sanctions, which by definition are extraterritorial in scope (that is, no state applies economic sanctions against itself). The Committee did not question the need for economic sanctions, nor the authority of the Security Council to impose them. Furthermore, the Committee also reaffirmed the principle that each state bears the primary responsibility for the protection and fulfillment of economic, social, and cultural rights. However, at the same time, the Committee used this opportunity to underscore the extraterritorial human rights obligations that states possess: "Just as the international community insists that any targeted State must respect the civil and political rights of its citizens, so too must that State and the international community itself do everything possible to protect at least the core content of the economic, social and cultural rights of the affected peoples of that State" (par. 7).

In addition to its treatment of extraterritorial obligations through the vehicle of its General Comments, the Committee has started to pursue this issue in other ways as well, especially in its response to the periodic reports of Western states. One of the examples Skogly makes reference to is the Committee's Concluding Observations to Ireland's 2002 treaty report. Employing the niceties of diplomatic discourse (of course), the Committee "encouraged" the Irish government, as a member of both the World Bank and the International Monetary Fund, to "do all it can to ensure that the policies and decisions of those organizations are in conformity with the obligations of States parties under the Covenant, in particular the obligations . . . concerning international assistance and cooperation." The Committee then "urged" Ireland to ensure that its contribution to international development cooperation reaches 0.45 percent of Gross National Product (GNP) by the end of 2002 "and that this annual figure increases as quickly as possible, to the United Nations target of 0.7 per cent of GNP." (Skogly 2006:152)

One final indication that extraterritorial obligations are a central feature of the International Covenant on Economic, Social and Cultural Rights comes from the work of the Special Rapporteur on the Right to Food (Jean Ziegler). Ziegler divides states' obligations into two categories: principal obligations and complementary obligations. According to his report to the Commission on Human Rights,

> Governments . . . have a duty to support the fulfillment of the right to food in poorer countries. Developing States that do not possess the necessary resources for the full realization of the right to food are obliged to actively seek international assistance, and wealthier States have a responsibility to help. This requires States, depending on the availability of their resources, to cooperate with other countries to support their fulfillment of the right to food. (Ziegler 2003: par. 56, citation omitted)

In sum, there is little question that the International Covenant on Economic, Social and Cultural Rights is replete with extraterritorial obligations that state parties are legally obligated to meet. The Covenant does not have the kind of language that is found in other human rights instruments that might be interpreted as restricting its scope to the "territory" and/or the "jurisdiction" of each state party. Furthermore, the Covenant is quite clear and succinct that the rights in the Covenant are to be met through "international assistance and cooperation" between the member states. This is what the framers intended, and this is why they used the language that they did. Nothing (or at least nothing in international law) could be any clearer than this. And finally, the U.N. Committee on Economic, Social and Cultural Rights, the authoritative source for interpreting the Covenant, has started to focus on the extraterritorial obligations of states and to press states on this issue.

Yet, despite all this, states continue to ignore the very existence of these obligations, at least as a matter of law. Thus, while many states do assist other countries and engage in a certain level of international cooperation and assistance, there is not a single state that does so on the basis that there is an international legal standard that demands this. Rather, even the most generous states view such matters as being completely within their own discretion. In short, states—all states—continue to act as if they do not have human rights obligations outside their own national borders. And it is for this reason—more than any other—that economic rights continue to be violated on such a massive scale.

However, one of the problems is what a state's obligation under the Economic Convention entails. You will recall from our discussion in the introduction concerning Henry Shue's approach: while human rights might be universal, no one state (and certainly no one person) has the obligation to meet all of those rights. Rather, what Shue talked about was "full coverage." The problem is that "full coverage" depends very much on what other states contribute—or fail to contribute. In that way, then, perhaps a better approach would be to establish some kind of benchmark, and the one that the U.N. Committee on Economic, Social and Cultural Rights employs is that a (developed) state is obligated to provide 0.7 percent of its Gross Domestic Product (GDP). Thus, as a working rule, an industrialized state has met its obligation under the Economic Covenant if it provides 0.7 percent of its GDP in foreign assistance to meet the human rights of "others."

International Covenant on Civil and Political Rights

Turning to the third leg of the International Bill of Rights, it was noted earlier that the International Covenant on Civil and Political Rights differed from the Economic Covenant in several ways. Most noteworthy is the seemingly restrictive language of Article 2 (1) of the Political Covenant: "Each State Party to the present Covenant undertakes to respect and to ensure to all individuals within its territory and subject to its jurisdiction the rights recognized in the Present Covenant." In addition to this, there is no mention in the Political Covenant of anything like the "international assistance and cooperation" language in the Economic Covenant.

Notwithstanding these differences, the Human Rights Committee (HRC), the U.N. treaty body that is the authoritative source for interpreting the Political Covenant, has not hesitated to give the Covenant an extraterritorial interpretation. The clearest example of this is the

Committee's decision in *Lopez v. Uruguay*, which we briefly looked at in the previous chapter. You will recall, the case involved an allegation of kidnapping of a Uruguayan national by Uruguayan officials—but in Argentina, not Uruguay. The Uruguayan government denied that the abduction had ever taken place, but in addition, it argued that the case should be ruled inadmissible because the event would have taken place outside the "territory" and "jurisdiction" of Uruguay, and thus, Uruguay would not be bound by the provisions of the Political Convention in this extraterritorial operation.

The Committee unanimously rejected this position. It held that what was key was the "relationship between the individual and the State in relation to a violation of any of the rights set forth in the Covenant, wherever they occurred." Furthermore, it ruled that Article 2 (1)

> places an obligation upon a State party to respect and ensure rights "to all individuals within its territory and subject to its jurisdiction," but does not imply that the State party concerned cannot be held accountable for violations of rights under the Covenant which its agents commit upon the territory of another State, whether with the acquiescence of the Government of that State or in opposition to it. (par. 12.3)

In an individual opinion, Christian Tomuschat voiced even stronger objection to the position espoused by the Uruguayan government, pointing out that this approach would lead to "utterly absurd results." Going further, Tomuschat writes, "Never was it envisaged . . . to grant States parties unfettered discretionary power to carry out willful and deliberate attacks against the freedom and personal integrity against their citizens abroad. Consequently, despite the wording of article 2 (1), the events which took place outside Uruguay come within the purview of the Covenant." (Communication No. R. 12/52)

The Human Rights Committee has continued to develop the principle of extraterritorial obligations, most notably in General Comment Number 31 (2004) where the HRC clearly stated that each State Party to the Political Covenant has an obligation to carry out the provisions of the Covenant not only within its own territorial borders but also far beyond that—literally.

> While article 2 is couched in terms of the obligations of State Parties towards individuals as the right-holders under the Covenant, *every State*

Party has a legal interest in the performance by every other State Party of its obligations. This follows from the fact that the "rules concerning the basic rights of the human person" are *erga omnes* obligations and that . . . there is a United Nations Charter obligation to promote universal respect for, and observance of, human rights and fundamental freedoms. Furthermore, the contractual dimension of the treaty involves any State Party to a treaty being obligated to every other State Party to comply with its undertakings under the treaty. (par. 2, emphasis supplied)

The Committee then went on to promote a vision of human rights that, it must be said, is vastly different from the manner in which states have viewed their international human rights obligations.

Accordingly, the Committee commends to States Parties the view that violations of Covenant rights by any State Party deserve their attention. To draw possible attention to possible breaches of Covenant obligations by other States Parties and to call on them to comply with their Covenant obligations should, far from being regarded as an unfriendly act, be considered as a reflection of legitimate community interest. (par. 2)

Sigrun Skogly has offered this observation of the enormous implications of this General Comment:

Thus . . . the Committee confirms that states have not only a legitimate interest but an *obligation* to show an interest in the human rights situation in other countries, and that this should not be considered undue interference. If we are to draw the logical conclusion from this assertion, it could safely be argued that it is in the legal interest of a state to consider the human rights situation of individuals in other states, it will be even more pertinent for the first state to consider its own influence upon the human rights enjoyment of individuals in those states. (Skogly 2006: 154, emphasis in original)

Unfortunately, states have seldom (if ever) concerned themselves (at least publicly) with whether other member countries are performing their obligations under the Political Covenant—or any other human rights treaty for that matter. More than this, states have systematically turned a blind eye to whether their own actions are having a positive or negative effect on the enjoyment of human rights in other countries. The larger point is this. There are two essential reasons that massive levels of human rights violations continue to exist. The first reason is the most obvious: there continue to be a large number of governments that simply do not respect the human rights of their own citizens. The second reason is less obvious but no less important: not only have "outside" states shown only sporadic interest in human rights practices elsewhere (and, invariably, only to the extent of simply condemning the practices of other states), but also they have shown virtually no interest in understanding how their own actions might affect the human rights protection of other people.

OTHER "HARD LAW" INSTRUMENTS

In the section that follows this, I will make the argument that *all* of international human rights law is based on extraterritorial principles. In other words, when a country becomes a member of *any* international human rights treaty—the International Convention on the Elimination of All Forms of Racial Discrimination, the Convention on the Elimination of All Forms of Discrimination against Women, and so on—it is thereby agreeing to be part of an international effort to address whatever human rights problem is the focus of that particular treaty. Before turning to this, however, it will be helpful to examine extraterritorial obligation provisions in other international human rights instruments.

Torture Convention

One of the more interesting aspects of the Torture Convention is its mix of restrictive and broad language. Article 2 (1) is an example of the former: "Each State Party shall take effective legislative, administrative, juridical or other measures to prevent acts of torture in any territory under its jurisdiction." As noted with regard to the Political Covenant, this kind of language ("territory" and "jurisdiction") might suggest that the only obligations that state parties have is within their respective domestic realms.

On the other hand, the scope of the Torture Convention is arguably as wide as can be found in any international human rights treaty in the sense that a number of its provisions demand that state parties not only concern themselves with human rights conditions and practices in other states but also that each state party play no role in "aiding and assisting" such violations (or even the possibility of such violations). Certainly, the most noteworthy provision is the prohibition in Article 3 against returning a person to a country where there is a likely prospect that this person will be tortured: "No State party shall expel, return (refouler) or extradite a person to another State where there are substantial grounds for believing that he would be in danger of being subjected to torture."

Several things need to be said about this provision. The first is that although the sending state would not actually be engaging in carrying out any of the torture itself, its own action in returning someone to a state where that person *might* be tortured is, by itself, a violation of the Torture Convention. The second thing is that the violation occurs at the moment that the return is effectuated, not when torture is actually carried out. This leads to the final point, which is that the violation occurs even if no torture occurs. Rather, the "wrong" of the sending state is returning a person to a country where there are substantial grounds for believing that this person might be tortured.

Another aspect of the Torture Convention with enormous extraterritorial obligations implications is its provision regarding universal jurisdiction. Under Article 5 (1) a state "shall take such measures as may be necessary to establish its jurisdiction" over persons who direct or commit or conspire to commit torture, whenever (1) the offenses are committed in any territory under its jurisdiction or on board a ship or aircraft registered in that state; (2) the alleged offender is a national of that state; or (3) the victim is a national of that state if that state considers it appropriate. Beyond this, however, Paragraph 2 widens states' obligations even further: "Each State Party shall likewise take such measures as may be necessary to establish its jurisdiction over such offences in cases where the alleged offender is present in any territory under its jurisdiction and it does not extradite him."

What this paragraph means, quite simply, is that when a person who has allegedly directed or carried out torture is within a state party's territorial borders—whether this person is a national of that country or not; whether the victim is a national of this country or not; and whether this torture was carried on within this state's territorial borders or not—this state party has a legal obligation to either prosecute this alleged torturer or else it must extradite him to another country that will prosecute him.

The final extraterritorial provision in the Torture Convention that will be noted is the inter-state complaint system created in Article 21.

Under this provision one state party can file a complaint with the U.N. Committee against Torture when it has reason to believe that another state party "is not fulfilling its obligations under this Convention." In that way, the Torture Convention not only obligates states to be concerned with human rights practices in other states, but it provides a mechanism where this might be accomplished.

To summarize, the Torture Convention not only sets forth a host of domestic obligations for states (prohibiting torture, investigating allegations of torture, providing a remedy for those who have been tortured, and so on), but it also contains a number of extraterritorial obligations for state parties as well. What is clear—is it not?—is that when a country becomes a party to the Torture Convention it is not only committed to eliminating torture domestically, but it is also making a pledge to be part of an international force that seeks to address the scourge of torture—no matter where this takes place.

In actual practice, however, the Torture Convention looks completely different from any of this. As empirical data has shown, being a party to this (or any other) international human rights treaty has essentially no bearing on actual state practice. In that way, countries that are a state party to the Torture Convention are just as likely—seemingly more likely—to carry out torture than those that are not (Hathaway 2002).

This, of course, represents a monumental failure of international law. However, what is less obvious but of equal importance is that "other" states—even states that do not lay a hand on their own citizens—have also failed to meet their international obligations. For one thing, not a single inter-state complaint has ever been filed under the Torture Convention. Certainly, this cannot be because torture has been eliminated. On a slightly more encouraging note, there have been a few instances where "outside" states have sought to prosecute foreign nationals who have directed or carried out torture—with the international effort to extradite and prosecute former Chilean dictator Augusto Pinochet serving as the prime example. Still, it also has to be said that such efforts have been very few and far between, and thus, virtually all those who directed or carried out torture are as free outside their countries as they are at home. It is estimated, for example, that there are literally hundreds of former torturers now residing in the United States. To be clear, as a state party to the Torture Convention, the United

States has a legal obligation to either "prosecute or extradite" each one of these people. Thus, the United States has failed to meet the legal standard established under the Convention. However, the United States is in "excellent" company because every other country that is a state party to the Torture Convention has essentially ignored this same legal obligation as well.

In short, the Torture Convention has changed very little. States continue to torture. Amnesty International estimates that torture is practiced in more than 160 countries in the world. Although this is deeply disturbing it is by no means surprising. However, what receives almost no attention is the fact that other states have done almost nothing to try to stop these practices. The point is that states that practice torture are violating international law, but so are the states that do not try to lift a finger to prevent this. It is simply not a matter of which action (or inaction) is "worse." Rather, all state parties have agreed to be bound by certain legal obligations, and yet, in different ways, all have failed to meet these obligations.

Convention on the Rights of the Child

The most widely adopted international human rights treaty is the Convention on the Rights of the Child (Children's Convention). Like all other international human rights treaties, the Children's Convention not only obligates states to act in a certain manner domestically, but it sets forth extraterritorial obligations for the member states as well. These extraterritorial obligations are most clearly spelled out in Article 4:

> State Parties shall undertake all appropriate legislative, administrative, and other measures for the implementation of the rights recognized in this Convention. In regard to economic, social and cultural rights, State Parties shall undertake such measures to the maximum extent of their available resources and, where needed, within the framework of *international cooperation.* (emphasis supplied)

If some of this language sounds familiar it should. Skogly explains that the drafters purposely copied the "international cooperation" language and approach of the Economic Covenant. She notes that throughout the drafting of the Children's Convention there was a "strong commitment" toward the need for international cooperation and that this point was not the least bit controversial. With respect to Article 4 in particular, she writes, "The drafters of the Convention on the Rights of the Child considered international cooperation (including assistance) to be of fundamental importance, and it was taken for granted that it was included in the text throughout the drafting period" (Skogly 2006: 104).

I do not mean to belabor the point, but since this very issue continues to be systematically ignored or misinterpreted, perhaps overkill is not the problem. What Article 4 means is that state parties have the "principal" or "primary" responsibility to protect the rights of children living within the territorial boundaries of that country but that there might be instances where these efforts are not sufficient to meet those rights. In those instances, outside states will also have to attend to the protection of those rights.

Let's say that large numbers of children in Nepal are not receiving an education, in contravention of Article 28 of the Children's Convention. The primary responsibility for educating children in that country rests with the Nepalese government, which, for whatever reason, is failing to meet its obligation. In that way, the Nepalese government is in violation of its obligations under international law.

This, however, does not end matters—although state practice would seem to suggest otherwise. "Outside" states have an obligation to protect the human rights of these children as well. This is why the drafters of the Children's Convention included the language "international cooperation." Yet, what does "international cooperation" mean? The first thing to note is what it does *not* mean. This obligation does not mean that other state parties can arrive in Nepal, uninvited and unannounced, and start to build schools and run classes in that country. Such actions would constitute an infringement on Nepal's territorial sovereignty. However, this still does not negate the fact that these other member states have undertaken a legal obligation to help ensure that children in Nepal receive an education. Perhaps the problem is one of resources, and thus, foreign assistance has to be provided. Or maybe diplomatic initiatives have to be undertaken with the Nepalese government. It might also be that the policies and practices of international financial institutions have to be modified or changed. The point is that the right to education is universal—but so is the obligation to meet this right. The failure to meet this right constitutes an international wrong on the part of the government of Nepal. However, it also constitutes a "wrong" on the part of the other member states as well. The Children's Convention demands "international cooperation"—the language here is clear—and state parties have a legal obligation to meet this standard.

Genocide Convention

Article 1 of the Genocide Convention provides, "The Contracting Parties confirm that genocide, whether committed in peace or in time of war, is a crime under international law which they undertake to prevent and punish." There are two ways of interpreting this language. The first is that a member state's legal duty is solely a domestic one. In other words, each state has a duty—against itself—to "prevent and punish" acts of genocide. The other reading of this language is that each state party has a legal obligation to ensure that genocide does not occur (and a duty to punish those responsible if and when it does occur)—not only within its own territorial borders but in all other countries as well. Certainly, the second reading provides a far more natural reading and one that is far more consistent with the object and purpose of the Genocide Convention itself. And much to their collective credit, states have adopted the second reading.

However, much to their collective discredit, states have done something equally insidious. What they have done, systematically, is to refuse to recognize genocide when it has occurred. The 1994 genocide in Rwanda serves as a prime example of this phenomenon where states made every imaginable effort to avoid describing the genocide in that country as constituting "genocide." William Schabas writes,

> What is known is that several members of the Security Council, and in particular the permanent members, were extremely reluctant to use the word "genocide" in a resolution directed to the Rwandan crisis. In the view of many, including the Secretary-General Boutrous Boutrous-Ghali, this was because a finding of genocide would impose an obligation to act to prevent the crime. The United States was foremost among those who were uncomfortable with the word genocide. At a press briefing on 10 June 1994, State Department spokeswoman Christine Shelley said that the United States was not prepared to declare that genocide was taking place in Rwanda because "there are obligations which arise in connection with the use of the term." (Schabas 2000: 495)

In what appears to be a reversal, at least with respect to U.S. policy, President George W. Bush has acknowledged the genocide in the Sudan as exactly that: "genocide." Unfortunately, however, this has done nothing to prompt any kind of American action.

Two points need to be made. The first is that there is a legal duty to "prevent and punish" the crime of genocide and failure to either "prevent" or "punish" constitutes a violation of international law. Is this failure as bad as the act of genocide itself? Of course it is not. On the other hand, the Genocide Convention does establish a legal standard that needs to be recognized and enforced. This leads to the second point, which is that international legal standards also apply to the manner in which states seek to "prevent or punish." Most noteworthy in this regard is the fact that when the French government finally did intervene in Rwanda, it did so in a manner that violated the Genocide Convention. France's intervention (Operation Turquoise) was based on protecting its Hutu allies—those responsible for carrying out the genocide. In that way, France provided "aid and assistance" to acts of genocide, and thus, it should be held accountable for doing so.

Refugee Convention

The Refugee Convention provides for both extraterritorial and territorial obligations, although it is oftentimes less than clear where one begins and the other one ends. The clearest example where a state exercises "territorial" power is when refugee claimants are within the territory of the receiving state and this state is bound by certain international human rights standards (under the Refugee Convention itself, but also under general international law) that serve to protect these foreign nationals—such as access to courts or the right to an education.

Yet, there are a number of ways where this situation becomes muddled and where the distinction between those things "extraterritorial" and those things "territorial" begins to break down. For one thing, visa restrictions have served as a way in which receiving states are able to exercise a form of extraterritorial control that serves to prevent individuals from leaving their country of origin in the first place, thereby averting refugee situations altogether. These efforts are oftentimes carried out by the would-be receiving state, placing its own officials in the would-be sending state to effectuate this policy. Is this territorial, extraterritorial—or both? Another way in which this distinction breaks down is that states are increasingly resorting to the use of refugee processing centers outside their own borders when making refugee determinations. Examples of extraterritorial refugee processing include the American policy of using Guantanamo Bay, Cuba, to process asylum claims of Haitian boat people as well as Australia's so-called Pacific Solution, where Afghan asylum claimants have been held on the island of Nauru. Beyond this, several European countries (most notably, the United Kingdom, Denmark, Germany, and Italy) have already explored options for creating refugee processing centers in various places outside of Europe. In that way, asylum applicants are physically removed from the state where they are seeking refugee protection, but obviously, they are still subject to the "jurisdiction" of this state.

However, even when refugees or refugee claimants are physically present in the "receiving" state, the distinction between "territorial" and "extraterritorial" is less than clear. This is particularly the case in refugee campus. Even when these camps are physically within the territorial borders of the receiving state, this state seldom exercises anything approaching complete sovereign power over them. Instead, this state invariably shares power with various international organizations (especially the Office of the High Commissioner for Refugees) as well as any number of nongovernmental organizations. And for those living in these camps, there is little (if any) recourse or accountability when human rights violations do occur—either at the hands of the receiving state, the sending state itself, or as the result of policies pursued by the various nongovernmental organizations involved in refugee protection (Farmer 2006).

On the other hand, the clearest extraterritorial obligation is the prohibition against sending a person back to a country where this person would have a "well-founded fear" of persecution. This obligation is similar to the nonrefoulement provision in the Torture Convention that we looked at earlier, although there are some slight differences between these two provisions, especially the fact that the Torture Convention, unlike the Refugee Convention, does not demand that the fear of persecution be based on any of the five factors (race, religion, nationality, membership of a particular social group, or political opinion).

If nothing else, refugee protection should help call into question any clear and neat distinction between "territorial" and "extraterritorial." For one thing, the entire phenomenon of refugee protection, by definition, is based on the transnational (or extraterritorial) movements of people. In addition, and as we saw in the previous chapter, the idea that a country has no human rights obligations to a refugee claimant unless (and until) that person has reached its territory offers a strained reading, not only of the Refugee Convention itself, but also of international human rights law more broadly. But what is just as strange is the idea that a receiving state would have absolutely no human rights obligations toward any foreign nationals outside its territorial boundaries until the moment of arrival—at which point this state would now have sole responsibility for the protection of all human rights for these individuals. The better way to conceptualize refugee protection (but also human rights in general) is to think in terms of universal obligations but where there is a shift in terms of which state has the primary responsibility (but not the sole responsibility) for protecting human rights. Refugee protection represents a transfer of states' obligations. The receiving state now takes on primary responsibility for protecting human rights, and it does so based on the very fact that the refugee's home country refuses to do so. However, the point is that the (receiving) state always had (secondary) human rights obligations toward those outside (now inside) its borders.

GATT/WTO Obligations

The last of the "hard law" instruments we will look at are those governing international trade. Although the Generalized Agreement on Tariffs and Trade (GATT) and the World Trade Organization (WTO) are oftentimes seen as being the enemy in terms of human rights protection, what is noteworthy for our present purposes is that one of the primary goals of both GATT and WTO is to raise standards of living and to contribute to the progressive development of the economies of all involved countries, particularly developing and least-developed countries. Thus, these treaties demand that, "There is a need for positive efforts designed to ensure that developing countries, and especially the least developed among them, secure a share in the growth in international trade commensurate with the needs of their economic development." In short, these measures are intended to help protect human rights—not to achieve the opposite—and states have an extraterritorial obligation under these treaties to ensure this takes place.

"SOFT LAW" INSTRUMENTS

International human rights law is oftentimes demarcated between "soft" and "hard" law. The idea is that the former are less enforceable (or at least less enforced) than the latter. As I mentioned before, there is no part of international human rights law that truly is "enforced," so this seems like a distinction with little meaning. Still, I will maintain this distinction for purposes of simplicity. The more important point is that extraterritorial obligations are found not only in hard international human rights law but in soft law as well.

Right to Development

In December 1986 the United Nations General Assembly adopted the "Declaration on the Right to Development," proclaiming this to be an inalienable human right. The primary responsibility for meeting the right to development is the home state. In that way, this right is consistent with the entirety of international human rights law. However, the Declaration is also premised on the notion that the right to development cannot be met without the assistance and cooperation of the entire international community. This, too, is consistent with the entirety of international human rights law. The Preamble begins with this language: "Bearing in mind the purposes and principles of the Charter of the United Nations relating to the achievement of *international co-operation* in solving *international problems* of an economic, social, cultural or humanitarian nature . . ." (emphases supplied). Furthermore, Article 3 (3) reads,

> States have the *duty to co-operate* with each other in ensuring development and eliminating obstacles to development. States should realize their rights and fulfill their duties in such a manner as to promote a new international economic order based on sovereign equality, interdependence, mutual interest and co-operation among all States, as well as to encourage the observance and realization of human rights. (emphasis supplied)

Article 4 (1) repeats this same theme: "States have the duty to take steps, *individually and collectively*, to formulate international development policies with a view of facilitating the full realization of the right to development" (emphasis supplied). Finally, Article 6 (1) sets forth states' extraterritorial obligations once again: "All States *shall co-operate* with a view of promoting, encouraging and strengthening *universal* respect for and observance of human rights" (emphases supplied).

Millennium Declaration

Although the U.N. Millennium Declaration would fall into the category of "soft" law, there certainly is no clearer expression of how and why human rights obligations transcend national borders. In language that borders on the poetic, the Millennium Declaration provides some measure of hope against actual state practice:

> We recognize that, in addition to our separate responsibilities to our individual societies, we have a collective responsibility to uphold the principles of human dignity, equality and equity at the global level. As leaders we have a duty therefore to all the world's people, especially the most vulnerable and, in particular, the children of the world, to whom the future belongs.

Undoubtedly the most significant result of this effort was the establishment of the Millennium Development Goals (MDGs). These are to (1) eradicate extreme hunger and poverty, (2) achieve universal primary education, (3) promote gender equality and empower women, (4) reduce child mortality, (5) improve maternal health, (6) combat HIV/AIDS, malaria, and other diseases, (7) ensure environmental sustainability, and (8) develop a global partnership for development.

Meeting the MDGs by the target date of 2015 would certainly be a remarkable achievement (Alston 2005). However, this will most assuredly *not* happen if states continue to see their human rights obligations as extending no further than their own territorial borders. To date, notwithstanding all of the platitudes and sentiments about "collective responsibility" and a duty "to all the world's people," states continue to act as if they do not have a single human rights obligation outside their own national borders.

EXTRATERRITORIAL OBLIGATIONS
IN ALL HUMAN RIGHTS TREATIES

What we have looked at thus far are a number of international instruments that contain provisions that extend member states' human rights obligations beyond their own national borders. In some cases, such as the Economic Covenant and the Children's Convention, these obligations are spelled out quite clearly in the treaty itself. In other situations, most notably the Political Covenant, states' extraterritorial obligations are not readily evident from the language in the treaty, although it also has to be said that the Human Rights Committee, the authoritative source for interpreting the Political Covenant, has readily recognized that member states have extraterritorial obligations under this treaty.

I want to conclude this chapter by presenting two arguments. The first is that extraterritorial obligations are not only inherent in *all* international human rights but that extraterritorial obligations go to the very essence and reason for why international human rights treaties exist in the first place. As I stated earlier, if human rights protection was something that a state could do on its own, there simply would be no need to have any international human rights law. Rather, the human rights practices of each state would be governed by the law of that individual state. States, however, have thought otherwise. They have concluded (correctly) that human rights protection can only be met through international assistance and cooperation. The problem, quite simply, is that while states have had little problem recognizing the importance of acting together, they have had enormous difficulty in actually doing so. Even an act as simple and as straightforward as filing an inter-state complaint against a state that systematically tortures its own people is something that member states seem completely incapable of carrying out. The rationale that seems to be employed is that what goes on in other states is not the business of the rest of the international community. Yet, this is the very reason for why international human rights law exists in the first place.

The second point relates to how we view human rights, particularly what constitutes a violation of those rights. Notwithstanding the universality of human rights, and despite the existence of explicit provisions setting forth states' extraterritorial obligations, there is very little about international human rights law that truly is "international." Rather, all that we see—perhaps all that we are capable of seeing—are those violations that are carried out by someone else. This view of human rights must change. The degree to which states contribute to the destruction of human rights protection must come to be recognized, and states must be held accountable when their actions (or inactions) lead to this result. Finally, victims of human rights violations must be given the means to pursue their claim against the offending state(s). This, then, is our fourth and final step.

REFERENCES

Alston, Philip. 2005. "Ships Passing in the Night: The Current State of the Human Rights and Development Debate Seen though the Lens of the Millennium Development Goals." *Human Rights Quarterly* 27:755–829.

Farmer, Alice. 2006. "Refugee Responses, State-like Behavior, and Accountability for Human Rights Violations: A Case Study of Sexual Violence in Guinea's Refugee Camps." *Yale Human Rights & Development Law Journal* 9:44–84

Hathaway, Oona. 2002. "Do Human Rights Treaties Make a Difference?" *Yale Law Journal* 111:1935–2041.

Morsink, Johannes. 1999. *The Universal Declaration of Human Rights: Origins, Drafting, and Intent.* Philadelphia: University of Pennsylvania Press.

Schabas, William. 2000. *Genocide in International Law: The Crime of Crimes.* New York: Cambridge University Press.

Skogly, Sigrun. 2006. *Beyond National Borders: States' Human Rights Obligations in International Cooperation.* Antwerp, Belgium: Intersentia.

Ziegler, Jean. 2003. *Second Submission of the Special Rapporteur on the Right to Food of the United Nations Commission on Human Rights.* http://www.fao.org/righttofood/common/ecg/25409_en_Ziegler2.pdf

United Nations Instruments

Charter of the United Nations. June 26, 1945, 59 Stat. 1031, T.S. 993, 3 Bevans 1153, *entered into force* October 24, 1945.

Universal Declaration of Human Rights. G.A. res. 217A (III), U.N. Doc A/810 at 71 (1948).

Economic Rights

Committee on Economic, Social and Cultural Rights. General Comment 3: The Nature of States Parties' Obligations (Fifth session, 1990), U.N. Doc. E/1991/23, annex III at 86 (1991), reprinted in Compilation of General Comments and General Recommendations Adopted by Human Rights Treaty Bodies, U.N. Doc. HRI/GEN/1/Rev.6 at 14 (2003).

——. General Comment 8: The Relationship between Economic Sanctions and Respect for Economic, Social and Cultural Rights (Seventeenth session,

1997), U.N. Doc. E/C.12/1997/8 (1997), reprinted in Compilation of General Comments and General Recommendations Adopted by Human Rights Treaty Bodies, U.N. Doc. HRI/GEN/1/Rev.6 at 50 (2003).

——. General Comment 12: Right to Adequate Food (Twentieth session, 1999), U.N. Doc. E/C.12/1999/5 (1999), reprinted in Compilation of General Comments and General Recommendations Adopted by Human Rights Treaty Bodies, U.N. Doc. HRI/GEN/1/Rev.6 at 62 (2003).

——. General Comment 14: The Right to the Highest Attainable Standard of Health (Twenty-second session, 2000), U.N. Doc. E/C.12/2000/4 (2000), reprinted in Compilation of General Comments and General Recommendations Adopted by Human Rights Treaty Bodies, U.N. Doc. HRI/GEN/1/Rev.6 at 85 (2003).

Convention on the Rights of the Child. G.A. res. 44/25, annex, 44 U.N. GAOR Supp. (No. 49) at 167, U.N. Doc. A/44/49 (1989), *entered into force* September 2, 1990.

Declaration on the Right to Development. G.A. res. 41/128, annex, 41 U.N. GAOR Supp. (No. 53) at 186, U.N. Doc. A/41/53 (1986).

International Covenant on Economic, Social and Cultural Rights. G.A. res. 2200A (XXI), 21 U.N.GAOR Supp. (No. 16) at 49, U.N. Doc. A/6316 (1966), 993 U.N.T.S. 3, *entered into force* January 3, 1976.

Millennium Declaration. UN Doc. A/55/2 (September 8, 2000).

Civil and Political Rights

Convention against Torture and Other Cruel, Inhuman or Degrading Treatment or Punishment. G.A. res. 39/46 [annex, 39 U.N. GAOR Supp. (No. 51) at 197, U.N. Doc. A/39/51 (1984)], *entered into force* June 26, 1987.

Convention on the Prevention and Punishment of the Crime of Genocide. 78 U.N.T.S. 277, *entered into force* January 12, 1951.

Convention Relating to the Status of Refugees. 189 U.N.T.S. 150, *entered into force* April 22, 1954.

International Covenant on Civil and Political Rights. G.A. res. 2200A (XXI), 21 U.N. GAOR Supp. (No. 16) at 52, U.N. Doc. A/6316 (1966), 999 U.N.T.S. 171, *entered into force* March 23, 1976.

Human Rights Committee. General Comment 31: Nature of the General Legal Obligation on States Parties to the Covenant, U.N. Doc. CCPR/C/21/Rev.1/Add.13 (2004).

Optional Protocol to the International Covenant on Civil and Political Rights. G.A. res. 2200A (XXI), 21 U.N. GAOR Supp. (No. 16) at 59, U.N. Doc. A/6316 (1966), 999 U.N.T.S. 302, *entered into force* March 23, 1976.

Trade

Agreement Establishing the World Trade Organization. Done at Marrakesh, April 15, 1994, *entered into force* January 1, 1995.

General Agreement on Tariffs and Trade (1994). Done at Marrakesh, April 15, 1994, *entered into force* January 1, 1995.

STEP FOUR: REMEDY

If a visitor from Mars came to Earth and was shown the wealth of international human rights law that presently exists, our extraterrestrial (or is it extraterritorial?) visitor would think that it had landed on the perfect planet. What this Martian would think from reading this law is that *all* of the inhabitants on Earth are protected by a myriad of human rights including the right to education, the right to social security, the right to life, the right to housing, the right to clean water, the right to express one's opinion freely, the right to life, and so on.

Or consider one particular right: the right to be free from torture. No doubt, the visiting Martian would think that torture seldom, if ever, takes place anywhere on this planet. After all, not only is torture prohibited in any number of international and regional human rights instruments, but also states where torture is practiced have pledged themselves to investigate such allegations and to prosecute those responsible for directing and carrying it out.

But it is not simply the state where the torture takes place that has an obligation to address this issue. Rather, our Martian friend would have to be impressed with the way in which nation-states have come together to address this matter. Most noteworthy, state parties to the Torture Convention have created an international constabulary force where they have legally obligated themselves to either "prosecute or extradite" any and all torturers found within their own territorial borders—whether the torture took place in that same country or not, or even whether either the victim or the perpetrator was a national of that country. What the Martian might reasonably conclude from this is that those responsible for torture would essentially have no place to run. They obviously cannot hide at home because their own country has pledged to prosecute those who have directed or carried out torture, but they could also not hide any place else either, or at least not in the territory of another state party to the Torture Convention.

The reality, as we all know, is anything but this. Rather than living in a world where human rights violations no longer exist, such violations (including torture) are actually the norm and certainly anything but the exception. The reason for this is that all of the international human rights laws in the world have not—and will not—amount to anything without the means to enforce these laws. In that way, the gravest shortcoming of all (this much should be obvious) relates to the inability, or unwillingness, to enforce the international human rights law that already exists. How this can be changed is our fourth step and to my mind the most important one of all.

THE RIGHT TO AN "EFFECTIVE REMEDY"

The dearth of human rights enforcement cannot be blamed on the lack of attention to this matter in the law itself. Rather, human rights treaties detail the obligations that state parties have when violations take place (Shelton 2005). One example of this is Article 2 (3) of the Political Convention, which provides,

> Each State Party to the present Covenant undertakes:
> To ensure that any person whose rights or freedoms are herein recognized are violated shall have an effective remedy, notwithstanding that the violation has been committed by persons acting in an official capacity.

Despite legal directives such as this, two enormous problems have emerged. The first relates to domestic enforcement itself, and the problem, quite simply, is that the state that has violated human rights is the same entity that is primarily responsible for enforcing the law—against itself! This, of course, has almost never taken place, and there is absolutely no reason to think that it ever will occur with any greater frequency in the future. In short, domestic enforcement has been almost a complete non-starter, and unless something is done to drastically al-ter this situation human rights enforcement will remain virtually non-existent.

The second problem relates to international enforcement—or the almost complete lack of such enforcement. Note that there is nothing in the language of Article 3 (or in similar provisions in other international human rights treaties) that would exclude "outside" states from playing an important role in providing an "effective remedy" for those whose human rights have been violated in another state. Rather, "each state party" to the Political Covenant is to ensure that "any person" whose civil and political rights have been violated will be provided with an "effective remedy." Beyond this, not only is international or extraterritorial enforcement entirely consistent with the overall aim of international human rights law, but also in a number of instances (such as the "extradite or prosecute" language in the Torture Convention noted above) extraterritorial enforcement is *mandatory*. Yet, with only rare exception (such as in the *Pinochet* case), the international community has not only avoided carrying out this responsibility, but also countries have actively taken steps in the other direction.

What must be done? I will suggest three things, with my primary focus being on the third. The first is to change our conceptualization of human rights itself. For far too long the international community has been content with a theoretical concept of human rights that has been totally divorced from the cruel reality that these "rights" are systematically violated. This notion of "human rights" must be discarded immediately. A right without a remedy is simply no right at all—and it is time that the international community came to recognize this.

What is also needed is the explicit recognition that the denial of an "effective remedy" constitutes a separate and distinct violation of international human rights law. Thus, in the case of torture, the first violation is the torture itself; the second is the denial of the promised right of an effective remedy.

One thing that is important to note here is that it is not only the "home" country that can violate human rights in this fashion. Rather, "other" states can be responsible for denying a victim an "effective remedy" as well. As we will see in a moment, this is most commonly done when a country provides sovereign immunity protection to another state, which has committed some human rights violation. It is important to point out that this does not necessarily mean that sovereign immunity protection can never, or should never, be provided. States are free to continue this practice under the banner of international solidarity or sovereign equality, or whatever other principle they believe sovereign immunity protection stands for. However, when a country provides sovereign immunity protection to a state that has violated international human rights law—and in doing so denies a victim the right to an "effective remedy" as it is obligated to do under international human rights law—this state has engaged in its own violation of international law, and it should be held accountable for these actions.

The third and perhaps most important change that must come about is that individuals must be given the means of enforcing their own human rights. Human rights are about empowering people, not disempowering them even further by dangling in front of victims the promise of an "effective remedy"—but then not delivering on this promise either.

What is so often ignored is that there are few (if any) "places" where individuals can bring a clam for a violation of their human rights. To do so at home against the government that is responsible for carrying out the violation in the first place is only to risk further mistreatment. On the international plane, only states can bring an action before the International Court of Justice (ICJ), and human rights concerns have certainly not dominated the ICJ's modest docket. In fact, one of the most noteworthy ICJ decisions in recent years was *against* the protection of human rights. In the *Arrest Warrants Case* (*Congo v. Belgium*), the ICJ held that Belgium's attempt to exercise "universal jurisdiction" in order to prosecute a sitting government minister for various human rights violations was contrary to the principle of head of state immunity and, thus, was in violation of international law.

The International Criminal Tribunals for Rwanda (ICTR) and for Yugoslavia (ICTY) have offered at least some form of "remedy" in the nature of criminal prosecutions. Thus, a number of war criminals from both of these states have been prosecuted and imprisoned. Yet, war crimes from all other areas of the globe—not to mention human rights violations more generally—are still, by and large, left unaddressed. The newly established International Criminal Court (ICC) was designed to address this matter, at least with respect to war crimes. Unfortunately, however, the ICC has been very slow in getting started, and it remains unclear when the Court's first prosecution will take place.

In terms of international human rights law itself, several treaties (the Political Convention, the Torture Convention, and the Convention on Racial Discrimination) allow a state party to file a complaint against another state party—or what is commonly referred to as the inter-state complaint system. The rationale behind the inter-state complaint system is to help ensure that all state parties to an international human rights treaty carry out their obligations under this treaty. In that way, then, the inter-state complaint system could serve an important remedial purpose. Yet, as noted before, not a single inter-state complaint has ever been filed under any one of these treaties, which does not inspire an enormous amount of confidence in this procedure.

In addition to this, four international human rights treaties (the Political Covenant, the Torture Convention, the Convention on Racial Discrimination, and the Convention on Discrimination against Women) have provisions under which individuals are allowed to file a claim against a state—so long as the state has agreed to this. An example of this is the Political Covenant. The Optional Protocol to the International Covenant on Civil and Political Rights creates a system whereby aggrieved individuals in certain states (those that are party to the Optional Protocol) can file a complaint with the U.N. Human Rights Committee (HRC) for alleged violations of the Political Covenant (as of October 2005 there were 105 countries that are parties to the Optional Protocol). Although these individual complaint procedures are to be applauded for providing at least some means by which individuals can pursue their own claim, there are a number of limiting factors that also need to be noted. For one thing, the HRC does not operate as a judicial body as such. It does not hear any oral evidence, and its "rulings" are not judicial determinations. Beyond this, an even more serious problem is whether states abide by the decisions handed down by the HRC (Donoho 2006: 26).

Turning to the three regional human rights tribunals—the European Court of Human Rights (ECHR), the Inter-American Court of Human Rights, and the African Commission on Human and Peoples' Rights—these courts were established for the purpose of providing individuals the opportunity of holding their government in check. The results, however, are mixed.

The most important thing to note is that not all "regions" of the world have a regional human rights tribunal. Beyond that, in terms of the existing courts, the African Commission has yet to make a serious impression, and African governments have almost nothing to fear from this body (Mutua 1999). The Inter-American Court has certainly achieved much more than this, and it has issued several noteworthy opinions. However, there have been at least two problems with the Court's work. The first relates to the Court's focus on the individual claimant at the expense of seeking to prevent future human rights violations (LaPlante 2004). The second problem, which certainly is related to the first, has been the active resistance of many of the Latin American states to the Court's rulings (Donoho 2006).

Of the three regional human rights tribunals, there is no question that the European Court of Human Rights has achieved the greatest degree of success, perhaps best evidenced in the hundreds of cases that the ECHR now hands down each year, thereby placing various governmental practices under microscopic analysis. In terms of the protection of human rights *within* Europe, the ECHR has done a fairly remarkable job—although it continues to be vexed by "serious" human rights violations (i.e., summary executions and torture) that arise from situations of war in states such as Russia and Turkey.

Yet, as we have seen before in our discussion of the *Bankovic* case and as we will see again in a moment in our analysis of another ECHR ruling (*Al-Adsani v. United Kingdom*), what can seriously be questioned is whether the ECHR is a human rights institution in the truest and broadest sense of that term. The reason for saying this is that the Court has given a clear indication that it will generally not engage itself in human rights violations that take place *outside* of "Europe"—even in instances involving the practices of European states, or in situations involving human rights violations carried out against European citizens.

In sum, although there have been some encouraging developments, it still can be said with a great deal of certainty that the overwhelming majority of individuals who are denied human rights protection simply have no place to go to press their claim. What follows are several different proposals that seek to address this situation. The first is the call for the creation of an International *Civil* Court. The second is a recent proposal for the creation of a World Court within the United Nations. The last proposal calls for using already existing domestic courts—only the courts outside the country where the human rights violation has taken place.

An International Civil Court

A few years ago I wrote an article proposing the creation of a permanent International *Civil* Court in The Hague, and I will take a short time to run through this argument (Gibney 2002). At that time (and at the present time as well), I had a number of concerns with the International Criminal Court that was then being proposed and that eventually came into existence in the summer of 2002. One problem is that the Criminal Court does nothing to provide individuals with the means or the ability of protecting their own human rights. Instead, this power continues to remain in the hands of someone else—in this case with the prosecutorial office of the International Criminal Court. A second problem is that the International Criminal Court only addresses a small fraction of human rights, its jurisdiction being limited to four international crimes: genocide, crimes against humanity, war crimes, and the crime of aggression. What remain untouched, then, are the vast bulk of human rights violations suffered by people the world over. Finally, the International Criminal Court only allows actions to be taken against individuals, but it purposely excludes proceedings against states. There is nothing wrong (and much that is right) with holding individuals responsible for violating human rights. However, there is nothing wrong (and a great deal that is right) with also holding states accountable. After all, individuals who are accused of these international crimes are almost always state actors. Why, then, should the state itself escape any and all responsibility for these matters?

Thus, the International Civil Court that I proposed would attempt to address each of these shortcomings. For one thing, the jurisdiction of an International Civil Court would be the entirety of human rights, and not simply those four crimes provided for under the Rome Statute creating the International Criminal Court. The rationale, as I explained above, is that something is not a "right" without the ability or the means to enforce it. Thus, what is needed is some mechanism for enforcing the entirety of international human rights law.

A second difference is that individuals would be able to enforce their own human rights and not be dependent on some other entity for this. Thus, what I envision is an International Civil Court where individuals (along with their legal representatives) who are victims of human rights violations would actually be able to initiate proceedings themselves and not have to rely on some other party, or the state itself, to do this for them. Human rights protection is simply too important to be left to the vagaries and the political persuasions of others.

The final difference would be that, while the International Civil Court would allow legal proceedings to be brought against individuals, its primary concern would be to hold states accountable for their actions. Note that under the view of state responsibility that I am proposing, this might entail an action being brought against several states. Thus, if State A tortures one of its citizens, this person should be able to bring an action before the International Civil Court against State A (as well as the individual state actors who directed or carried out this torture). In addition, however, let's say that State B provided torture equipment to State A (with close to full knowledge of how this equipment would be used) and agents of State C had "trained" agents of State A. What I am arguing is that the torture victim should also be able to use the International Civil Court to sue State B and State C for their own role in facilitating this egregious crime.

How would the International Civil Court operate? The answer is quite simple: just like any other civil court. Thus, aggrieved individuals (as a class or individually) would present evidence (written as well as oral), and states and individuals accused of carrying out such human rights violations would have the ability of contesting those accusations. The International Civil Court would then render a decision and issue a judgment.

As I stated at the outset, human rights are not complicated, nor should they be made to be complicated. The International Civil Court would be based on the most basic, and the most universal, notions of justice (Donovan and Roberts 2006). What the International Civil Court would seek to achieve is to provide full human rights protection for all human beings. Human rights protection would no longer remain in the realm of the theoretical or the aspirational. Rather, and arguably for the very first time, "universal" human rights might actually become just that.

A World Court

Manfred Nowak, the U.N. Special Rapporteur on Torture, has recently proposed the creation of a World Court of Human Rights (Nowak 2007). The Court would be based on a new international treaty—the Statute of the World Court of Human Rights—that would enter into force after a sufficient number of states had ratified the treaty. However, under this proposal each country would be able to choose which of the international human rights treaties the World Court would be able to exercise jurisdiction over them. For example, although a state might be party to a number of human rights treaties, it might choose to limit the World Court's jurisdiction to only one or a few of these treaties, with the idea being that this list could be expanded (or, presumably, contracted) at some future point in time. Another novel feature to Nowak's proposal is that non-state parties such as inter-governmental organizations (World Bank, NATO, WTO, and so on) and transnational corporations could also become parties to the treaty.

There is a great deal to admire about Nowak's proposal. For one thing, it clearly recognizes how deficient the international human rights regime has been in terms of providing an effective remedy to victims of human rights abuse. In addition, the proposal is intended to fit within the existing United Nations human rights framework. Finally, the World Court is intended to be exactly that—a court—whose decisions would be binding on those that are party to the new Convention.

There are, however, a few shortcomings to this proposal that should be mentioned. One is giving states the ability to determine whether the law will be made applicable to them. In my view, becoming a state party to an international human rights treaty means that a country already has decided to be bound by international law—not that it might think about it. A second weakness is that the proposal makes no attempt to change the law on state responsibility. This would simply perpetuate the current situation where international law only recognizes "direct" human rights violations but almost systematically ignores any and all "indirect" violations, such as "aiding and assisting." As I have explained earlier (chapter 2), this maintains a myopic view of human rights. Still, these concerns are minor. A World Court such as this would represent an enormous leap forward in terms of human rights protection, and such a proposal should be given very serious consideration.

Domestic Courts in Outside States

Perhaps the biggest problem with these two proposals is that both would necessitate creating new international institutions, something that is not easily undertaken, never mind accomplished. The final proposal is based on using already existing domestic courts—only the domestic courts of outside states. It is noteworthy that there is already strong precedent for this kind of thing in terms of the Alien Tort Statute litigation in the United States, where human rights victims have been able to pursue claims against individuals who directed and/or carried out abusive practices against them (Stephens and Ratner 1996). Where the present proposal differs is that its main target would be human rights–abusing states, rather than individuals. We now turn to two cases where this has been attempted.

Saudi Arabia v. Nelson

Saudi Arabia v. Nelson (1993) is based on a case brought by Scott Nelson, a U.S. citizen who was recruited in the United States to work for a state-run hospital in Saudi Arabia. Nelson's claim was that after registering a complaint about safety conditions with hospital authorities, he was imprisoned and tortured by Saudi security personnel. After his eventual release and return to the United States, Nelson brought suit against the Saudi government in federal district court. The case eventually made its way to the U.S. Supreme Court, which held that none of the exceptions in the Foreign Sovereign Immunity Act (FSIA) applied, and therefore, Saudi Arabia was protected against Nelson's suit.

By way of some background, for centuries states had enjoyed "absolute" immunity. What this means is that no state could be held accountable in the courts of another state for any of its actions. The reasoning behind the principle of absolute immunity was that all states are sovereign equals, and as sovereign equals one state should not be placed in a position of having to answer to another state. However, sovereign immunity has changed a great deal over the course of the past century or so, particularly as states have engaged in more nontraditional "commercial" practices. Thus, many states have come to adopt what has come to be known as the "restrictive" theory of sovereign immunity, which means that they are willing to provide a much more limited form of sovereign immunity.

The Foreign Sovereign Immunity Act is an example of this restrictive theory. Under FSIA, a foreign state being sued in American court will be granted sovereign immunity protection unless one of the listed exceptions is found to be applicable. The exceptions in the original Act included such things as the following: the state had waived immunity; the state had engaged in a "commercial activity" in the United States; the state had violated property rights (i.e., expropriation) in violation of international law; and the state had committed a "tortious act" in the United States.

An additional sovereign immunity exception was added in 1996 through passage of the Antiterrorism and Effective Death Penalty Act (AEDPA), which we briefly looked at earlier, for actions against states that have caused "personal injury or death that was caused by an act of torture, extrajudicial killing, aircraft sabotage, hostage taking, or the provision of material support or resources . . . for such an act." While this might sound like a general "human rights exception," it is not. For one thing, only U.S. nationals are able to invoke this exception. In addition, this exception only applies against the handful (literally) of states that have been designated by the U.S. State Department as a "state sponsor of terrorism." This original list of "state sponsors of terrorism" consisted of the "seven deadly sinners": North Korea, Syria, Cuba, the Sudan, Libya, Iraq, and Iran. Since then, however, Iraq and Libya have been removed from this list. To be clear, what this means is that those states that commit gross and systematic human rights violations but are not on this list (including the likes of Saudi Arabia) will continue to receive sovereign immunity protection in U.S. courts and under American law.

To return to *Nelson*, the sole issue addressed by the Court was whether the Saudi government had engaged in a "commercial activity" in the United States. If it did, sovereign immunity protection would be denied. However, if it did not, then Scott Nelson's suit would be dismissed because it would not fit into any one of the other FSIA exceptions for granting sovereign immunity. The justices were of differing minds, both in terms of whether the Saudi government had engaged in a "commercial activity" and whether such activity was carried out "within the United States." According to the majority opinion, the Saudi government had not engaged in a "commercial activity." Justice Souter writes, "The conduct boils down to abuse of power of its police by the Saudi Government, and however monstrous such abuse undoubtedly may be, a foreign state's exercise of the power of its police has long been understood for purposes of the restrictive theory as peculiarly sovereign in nature." 507 U.S. at 361.

Justice White and Justice Blackmun concurred in the result but based their opinion on the opposite conclusion, namely, that while the necessary "commercial activity" was present, such activity had not taken place in the United States. Finally, Justice Stevens' dissenting opinion argued that the Saudi government had not only carried out a commercial activity but that this activity had taken place within the United States. Thus, only Justice Stevens was of the mind that Saudi Arabia should not enjoy sovereign immunity under American law.

Nelson is (or at least should be) a discomforting decision. One aspect of this is simply the result in the case: a state that has carried out torture (against an American citizen no less) is granted sovereign immunity protection and allowed to escape any and all responsibility for its actions. But what is equally discomforting about the Court's approach is that international human rights law is virtually nowhere to be found, with the possible exception of Justice Souter's rather offhand remark, quoted earlier, describing the behavior of the Saudi government as "monstrous." Torture certainly is monstrous. But more than that, torture is illegal under both international and domestic (U.S.) law. Yet, the Court does not make any mention of this. Furthermore, torture is not simply a violation of international law, but also it is widely recognized as a *jus cogens* norm, which means that it is considered to be one of the most serious and egregious offenses in all of international law (along with such things as genocide and crimes against humanity). Yet, not a single opinion in *Nelson* alludes to this in any way. Furthermore, the Court never even begins to address the issue whether the United States, as a state party to the Torture Convention, has any obligations under international law and whether or not it has met those obligations.

Let me suggest two obligations and two violations. The first is the U.S. government's obligation to the international community more broadly (or what under international law is known as an obligation *erga omnes*). As a party to the Torture Convention, the United States has a responsibility to carry out its obligations under the treaty "in good faith." The point is that granting sovereign immunity protection to a state that practices torture is contrary to the object and purpose of the treaty, which is to eliminate torture and all its vestiges.

The second violation relates to the American treatment of Scott Nelson. Article 14 of the Torture Convention provides, "Each State Party shall ensure in its legal system that the victim of an act of torture obtains redress and has an enforceable right to fair and adequate compensation." The U.S. government has not ensured that a victim of torture obtains redress and possesses an enforceable right to fair and adequate compensation. Rather, through its actions, the United States has achieved just the opposite result. The response to this would be that Article 14 only applies to torture carried out within the territorial boundaries of the United States, and in fact, the U.S. government submitted an "understanding" to that effect when it ratified the Torture Convention. However, this is not a proper "understanding" of Article 14. The reason for saying this is that the language of Article 14 is much different than the language to be found in Article 13, which reads, "Each State Party shall ensure that any individual who alleges he has been subjected to torture in any territory under its jurisdiction has the right to complain to, and to have his case promptly and impartially examined by, its competent authorities." Thus, Article 14 does not contain any of the "territorial" and "jurisdictional" restrictions that can be found in Article 13—and no American "understanding" can change the clear language in the Torture Convention itself.

But the wrong committed by the Court goes much deeper than this. What the U.S. Supreme Court has done in *Nelson* is to simply ignore any and all of the broader issues relating to a state party's responsibilities under the Torture Convention, while at the same time it has focused almost exclusively on the mundane and the irrelevant. As it stands, *Nelson* is a case about what constitutes a "commercial activity in the United States"—and nothing more. However, what *Nelson* could have been—and what *Nelson* should have been about—is a case that not only addressed the issue of foreign sovereign immunity more generally (and the FSIA in particular) but also involved itself with the meaning of human rights and a state's responsibility to protect those rights. Unfortunately, there is not the slightest hint of this in *Nelson*.

One of the more useful things the Court might have done is to address the enormous inconsistencies to be found under U.S. law. Perhaps, it should not be surprising that one of the most glaring of these relates to the issue of territory. If Saudi officials had tortured Scott Nelson in the United States (that is, it had committed a "tortious act" in this country), or perhaps if it had tortured him on a ship sailing to the United States or an airplane headed to the United States, Saudi Arabia would not have received sovereign immunity protection. However, by torturing Nelson in Saudi Arabia, the Saudi state does receive sovereign immunity protection. This begs the question—does it not?—of why territory should matter like this. Why is torture by Saudi agents in Saudi Arabia deserving of sovereign immunity protection but torture by Saudi agents in Virginia not deserving of sovereign immunity protection? Beyond this, if the goal of sovereign immunity is to prevent one state from having to answer for its actions before the judicial branch in another state, in what way is this end achieved by this distinction of where the torture is carried out? Furthermore, if the goal of the Torture Convention is to eliminate the practice of torture, how is this end accomplished by granting sovereign immunity in one of these situations but not in the other?

Another issue that the Court could have addressed is whether providing sovereign immunity protection to a country that has violated a *jus cogens* norm is itself a violation of international law (Caplan 2003). It was this very question that was addressed by the European Court of Human Rights in its *Al-Adsani* decision, which we will turn to in a moment. However, the *Nelson* court never even mentions this issue.

Nelson was decided in 1993. As noted earlier, FSIA was amended in 1996 to include a seventh exception, but only for actions brought against a small number of states. The question is this: if a case like *Nelson* were to arise today, how would the Supreme Court decide such a case? My feeling is that it would apply the same kind of mechanical and simplistic distinctions that it did in *Nelson*—that is, the Court would simply refuse to address any of the bases of the law itself. The most obvious issue is how and why torture carried out by a country designated as a "state sponsor of terrorism" should be treated so differently from torture carried out by a state that is not designated as such. The ready answer, of course, is that Congress has created this seventh exception in order to address the scourge of international terrorism—and it is simply not the Court's role to question or to attempt to change what Congress has done.

Yet, two things have to be said in response. The first is to point out that there is no requirement in the law that the act in question (i.e., torture, hijacking) be carried out in furtherance of international terrorism. Thus, *all* torture carried out by the Cuban government (to choose one state and one transgression) would subject that government to suit in U.S. court—whether these acts of torture were in any way related to international terrorism or not. The second point is that *none* of the torture carried out by a state not so designated would subject this country to suit in American court—even if it could clearly be shown that the act in question related directly to international terrorism. Or to put this in a different context, because Afghanistan was not listed as a "state sponsor of terrorism" at the time of the September 11, 2001, attacks on the United States, the Afghan government would receive sovereign immunity protection in any suit for its "sponsorship" of these deadly attacks.

The larger point is that the Court's analysis is extraordinarily simplistic and incomplete. The only issue it seems capable of addressing is whether the actions of the Saudi government constituted a commercial activity (and, if so, whether that activity had occurred in the United States). What I am saying is that there is a completely different level of analysis that simply eludes the Court. The first relates to internal inconsistencies in FSIA itself. The second relates to whether FSIA is at all consistent with U.S. obligations under international law. The problem is that, in *Nelson*, the Supreme Court simply refuses to deal with either one of these issues.

Al-Adsani v. United Kingdom

Sulaiman Al-Adsani (the applicant) is a fighter pilot who had been living in the United Kingdom, but in 1991 he traveled to Kuwait to fight against the Iraqi invasion of that country. The applicant (who is a U.K.-Kuwait dual national) claimed that while in Kuwait he came into possession of some sex videotapes involving Sheikh Jaber Al-Sabah Al-Saud Al-Sabah ("the Sheikh"), who is related to the Emir of Kuwait. By some means, these tapes entered general circulation, for which the Sheikh held the applicant responsible. After the war was over, the Sheikh had the applicant tortured on two separate occasions. The second time, the applicant's head was repeatedly held under water in a swimming pool containing corpses. He was then dragged into a small room where the Sheikh set fire to a mattress soaked with gasoline and as a result the applicant suffered burns covering a quarter of his body surface. After receiving treatment in Kuwait, the applicant returned to England where he spent six more weeks in the hospital. In addition to his physical injuries, the applicant also suffered psychological damage. He claims that he has been diagnosed as suffering from a severe form of post-traumatic stress disorder that has been aggravated by death threats received after his return to England warning him not to take any action or give publicity to his situation.

On August 29, 1992, the applicant instituted civil proceedings in England for compensation against the Sheikh and the State of Kuwait in respect to the physical and mental harm suffered in Kuwait in May 1991 and threats against his life and well-being made after his return to the United Kingdom. The applicant was granted a default judgment against the Sheikh.

With respect to his claim against Kuwait, in an *ex parte* proceeding, the court initially found for the applicant, holding that there were a number of elements pointing to responsibility by the Kuwaiti state and further holding that the applicant had established a strong case for denying Kuwait sovereign immunity. After receiving the court's writ, the Kuwaiti government sought an order striking down these proceedings. The application was examined by the High Court on March 15, 1996, which delivered its judgment the same day. The court held that international law could only be used to assist in interpreting lacunae or ambiguities in a domestic statute, but when the terms of a statute were clear the statute was to prevail over international law. Section 1 (1) of the State Immunity Act of 1978 provides, "A State is immune from the jurisdiction of the courts of the United Kingdom except as provided in the following provisions of the Act," while Section 5 provides, "A State is not immune as respects proceedings in respect of (a) death or personal injury . . . caused by an act or omission in the United Kingdom." The court held that the grant of sovereign immunity was unambiguous—Kuwait had not brought about a death or injury in the United Kingdom—and, thus, there was no need to resort to international law for clarification. With respect to the applicant's claim of receiving death threats while in England, the court held that there was not enough evidence to hold Kuwait responsible for these threats. In sum, the court held that, for this action, Kuwait enjoyed sovereign immunity protection under British law, and the case against the Kuwaiti government was dismissed.

The applicant appealed the case to the Court of Appeals, which affirmed this holding. With respect to the applicant's argument that the prohibition against torture rose to the level of a *jus cogens* norm, thus overriding all other principles of international law, Lord Justice Stuart-Smith took the position that no authority was cited for this proposition. Stuart-Smith also maintained that those who drafted the legislation were certainly aware of the various international instruments regarding torture and that there was no apparent intent in the State Immunity Act to defer to this law.

In addition to these legal justifications, Lord Justice Stuart-Smith also pointed to the "dire" practical consequences of the applicant's submission:

> A vast number of people come to this country each year seeking refuge and asylum, and many of these allege that they have been tortured in the country whence they came. Some of these claims are no doubt justified, others are more doubtful. Those who are presently charged with the responsibility for deciding whether applicants are genuine refugees have a difficult enough task, but at least they know much of the background and surrounding circumstances against which the claim is made. The court would be in no such position. The foreign States would be unlikely to submit to the jurisdiction of the United Kingdom court, and in its absence the court would have no means of testing the claim or making a just determination. (cited in Al-Adrani, par. 18)

The other two members of the Court of Appeal likewise rejected the applicant's claim, although one (Lord Justice Ward) made the astute observation that "there may be no international forum (other than the forum of the *locus delicti* to whom a victim of torture will be understandably reluctant to turn) where this terrible, if established, wrong can receive civil redress." (cited in Al-Adrani, par. 18) In November 1996, the applicant was refused leave to appeal by the House of Lords, and his own purported attempts to obtain compensation from Kuwaiti authorities via diplomatic channels also proved to be unsuccessful.

Following this, on April 3, 1997, the applicant filed a claim against the United Kingdom claiming that, by granting sovereign immunity protection to Kuwait, the British government itself had violated several provisions of the European Convention: Article 3 (the right not to be tortured), Article 6 (the right to a fair trial), Article 1 (the obligation to secure human rights), and Article 13 (the right to an effective remedy). The decision by the ECHR is an uneasy attempt to reconcile what it readily concedes is an absolute prohibition against torture, on the one hand, with the notion of sovereign immunity, which it viewed as being a longstanding principle of international law. Thus, while recognizing that torture constitutes a peremptory (*jus cogens*) norm under international law, the Court still maintained the position that the U.K. had not violated the Convention in granting sovereign immunity to a state that practiced torture.

Article 3   Article 3 of the European Convention reads, "No one shall be subjected to torture or to inhuman or degrading treatment or punishment." The gist of the applicant's Article 3 claim is that this Article, when read in conjunction with Article 1 and Article 13, provides a right not to be tortured, and that the U.K. had failed to secure this right by granting Kuwait sovereign immunity in its courts. The Court acknowledged that Articles 1 and 3 do place a number of positive obligations on State Parties that are designed to prevent and provide redress for torture and other forms of ill-treatment. Through references to some of its own case law, the Court pointed out that these duties include the requirement that states take certain measures to ensure that individuals within their jurisdiction are not subjected to torture and also that a state must carry out a thorough and effective investigation of incidents of torture.

However, the Court severely limited the extent of these duties by positing that a "State's obligations applies only in relation to ill-treatment allegedly committed within its jurisdiction" (par. 38). This rule of territoriality notwithstanding, the Court referenced its landmark decision in *Soering v. United Kingdom* for the proposition that Article 3 has some "limited" extraterritorial application. The question raised in *Soering* was whether Great Britain would be in violation of the European Convention if it extradited a criminal defendant who was in British custody (Soering is a German national accused of committing a double murder in the state of Virginia) who, if convicted, faced the prospect of being placed on death row in Virginia (and, thus, suffer from what the Court termed the "death row phenomenon," which, in its view, violated Article 3 of the European Convention). The argument of the British government was that whatever human rights violations Soering would be subjected to would be as the result of acts performed by American officials on American soil. Thus, the British government argued that, if it were to extradite Soering, it would not be "responsible" for any harm that might then befall him.

Although the European Convention does not have a provision against nonrefoulement as does the Torture Convention and the Refugee Convention, the ECHR soundly rejected this position. Instead, it held that extradition under such circumstances would violate the "spirit and the intention" of Article 3 specifically and the European Convention more broadly.

By claiming that Article 3 has "limited" extraterritorial application, the *Al-Adsani* court was attempting to severely restrict its previous holding in *Soering*. Yet, it is not even clear that *Al-Adsani* is an "extraterritorial" case in the first place. Rather, the decision to provide Saudi Arabia sovereign immunity protection, and, at the same time, to deny an "effective remedy" to the applicant, is an act that was performed on British soil, carried out by British officials and under the rubric of British law. In other words, although the torture was performed on foreign soil, the decision to grant sovereign immunity protection was certainly carried out "within the territory and jurisdiction" of the United Kingdom.

The Court closed its Article 3 analysis by positing that the United Kingdom did not have any "causal connection" with the torture and that in these circumstances "it cannot be said that the High Contracting Party was under a duty to provide a civil remedy to the applicant in respect of torture allegedly carried out by the Kuwaiti authorities" (par. 40). What is so ironic is that this "causal connection" argument is essentially the same argument that the U.K. had made in *Soering*. However, the Court did find a "causal connection" in *Soering*, and it should have made a similar finding in *Al-Adsani* as well.

Article 6 The applicant also alleged that he was denied access to a court in the determination of his claim against the State of Kuwait and that this constituted a violation of Article 6 of the Convention, which provides, "In the determination of his civil rights and obligations or of any criminal charge against him, everyone is entitled to a fair and public hearing within a reasonable time by an independent and impartial tribunal established by law." The U.K. submitted that Article 6 (1) did not apply to the proceedings, and even if it did, any interference with the right of access to a court was compatible with its provisions.

The Court held that, while Article 6 was applicable, there was no indication that the United Kingdom was not in compliance with it. Rather, it ruled that the 1978 Act is in accord with the provisions of the 1972 European Convention on State Immunity (the Basle Convention), which itself was consonant with international law:

> Article 6 (1) of the Convention could not be interpreted so as to compel a Contracting State to deny immunity to and assert jurisdiction over a non-Contracting State. Such a conclusion would be contrary to international law and would impose irreconcilable obligations on the States that had ratified both the Convention and the Basle Convention. (par. 50)

Oddly enough, perhaps, the Court then immediately went on to state, "There were other, traditional means of redress for wrongs of this kind available to the applicant, namely diplomatic representations or an inter-State claim" (par. 50). The Court's position is that, although there is a general right to access to courts, this right is not absolute and is subject to "limitations," although such limitations will not be compatible with Article 6 (1) "if it does not pursue a legitimate aim and there is no reasonable relationship of proportionality between the means employed and the aim to be achieved" (par. 53). The Court concluded that British law met both criteria on the grounds that sovereign immunity is a generally accepted rule of international law.

The Court did acknowledge that the principle of sovereign immunity has come under increased attack. In that vein, it referenced the work of the International Law Commission, which has noted two exceptions to this principle, the first being the recent "terrorism" exception under U.S. law and the second being the *Pinochet* case, where the British High Court had held that a former head of state could be extradited for prosecution in a third state (Spain) for ordering and directing torture. The Court dismissed the former on the basis that the exception confirms the general rule. In other words, there would have been no need to create this new exception if human rights violations, generally, removed sovereign immunity protection. In terms of the *Pinochet* case, the ECHR distinguished the case before it on the basis that *Pinochet* should not be read to affect the immunity of states—only the immunity of individuals who were former heads of state. By way of conclusion, the Court held that while it was cognizant of the universal acceptance of the prohibition against torture, it was of the view that there is not yet "acceptance in international law of the proposition that States are not entitled to immunity in respect of civil claims for damages for alleged torture committed outside the forum State" (par. 66).

Concurring and Dissenting Opinions The *Al-Adsani* case elicited several noteworthy concurring and dissenting opinions. Judge Zupancic's concurring opinion focused on two matters. The first is that some of the duties under the Torture Convention are not compulsory. For example, Zupancic pointed to the language in Article 5 (1) (c), which provides, "Each State Party shall take such measures as may be necessary to establish its jurisdiction over [torture]. . . . When the victim is a national of that State *if that State considers it appropriate*" (emphasis in original). In Zupancic's view, while the United Kingdom might have allowed Al-Adsani's suit against Kuwait to proceed, it was not under any legal obligation to do so.

The second point is that the Court must take into account what Judge Zupancic termed "realistic" and "practical" considerations, the fear being that an opposite result would open up European courts to all sorts of human rights claims. Judge Pellonpaa's concurring opinion (joined by Judge Bratza) focused on this same issue. Pellonpaa quoted widely from the opinion of British trial court judge Stuart-Smith, who had claimed that a holding for Al-Adsani would lead to "dire consequences." Echoing this theme, Pellonpaa writes,

> The somewhat paradoxical result, had the minority's view prevailed, could have been that precisely those States which so far have been the most liberal in accepting refugees and asylum seekers, would have had imposed on them the additional burden of guaranteeing access to a court for the determination of perhaps hundreds of refugees' civil claims for compensation for alleged torture.

Pellonpaa continues with this approach by referring to the "lessons" to be learned from the case.

> In my view this case leaves us with at least two important lessons. First, although consequences should not alone determine the interpretation of a given rule, one should never totally lose sight of the consequences of a particular interpretation one is about to adopt. Secondly, when having to touch upon central questions of general international law, this Court should be very cautious before taking upon itself the role of a forerunner.

The joint dissenting opinion of Judges Rozakis and Caflisch (joined by Judges Wildhaber, Costa, Cabral Barreto, and Vajic) was based on the idea that there is either a hierarchy of international law—with *jus cogens* norms at the apex—or there is not. In that way, the majority opinion is strongly criticized for allowing a *jus cogens* norm (the prohibition against torture) to be trumped by the lower-level principle of sovereign immunity.

Judge Ferrari Bravo's dissenting opinion begins by exclaiming, "What a pity!" The basis of this dissent is that the Court simply needed to uphold the thrust of the House of Lords' judgment in the *Pinochet* case.

Putting on a brave face, Judge Ferrari Bravo closes on an optimistic note: "There will be other cases, but the Court has unfortunately missed a very good opportunity to deliver a courageous judgment."

Finally Judge Loucaides' dissenting opinion sharply criticizes the majority's attempt to draw a distinction between criminal law—where the *jus cogens* norm trumps the principle of sovereign immunity—and civil proceedings, where (apparently) it does not. In addition, Loucaides takes the position that any form of blanket immunity, without regard to any considerations connected with the specific proceedings, is wrong and that this is especially the case involving allegations of a violation of a peremptory norm of international law.

Analysis Although the result in *Al-Adsani* might seem like a "pity" or as a lost opportunity to render a "courageous judgment" (the same could be said for *Nelson* as well), perhaps the enormous implications of the decision could be better understood if one thinks about what the world would look like if the ECHR had reached the opposite result—that is, if the Court had ruled 9-8 in favor of Al-Adsani's claim, rather than 9-8 against him. My own view is that a ruling against Kuwait in this case would have immediately transformed the entirety of international human rights law from what exists at present. The reason why I say this is that victims of human rights violations would now have both a forum (domestic courts) as well as a reachable target (their own state).

The members of the Court might well have been aware of this, but they were even more concerned with what they felt would be the severe dislocations of an opposite holding. I want to discuss two of these "consequences." The first is the purported overload problem, variously described in such terms as "dire consequences" or "practical" or "realistic" considerations. There is no question that the European Court of Human Rights (which already has what amounts to an overwhelming caseload) has a valid concern with "numbers." Indeed, we saw the same rationale used in *Bankovic*, where the Court expressed the fear that an opposite holding would lead to a situation where "anyone in the world adversely affected" would attempt to file a claim against the European states.

There is no denying that there are literally millions of victims of human rights abuse in the world and, thus, millions of potential claimants. Still, what does not follow from this is the rather summary dismissal of a particular applicant's claim. For one thing, it is by no means clear that these countless victims will wish to pursue a claim against the offending state. Furthermore, what also is never considered by the Court is whether there are judicial mechanisms, most notably class action lawsuits, which might be used that would help address any overload problems (Van Schaack 2003).

Beyond this, the Court works under the assumption that human rights violations will always remain at their present level and that it is unfair or unwise to place a burden on the domestic courts of these European states to serve as a forum for these violations. What I question is this basic assumption. As I have said earlier, I am convinced that the primary reason human rights violations are carried out with impunity is that states that violate international human rights law have been able to do so—with impunity! Change this—begin to hold states accountable for their violations—and this equation would change almost immediately. Would a state continue to torture if there was a strong likelihood that torture victims would be able to bring a cause of action against this state in the court of another country and win a large monetary judgment? Some states might, but I would also suggest that, after a short period of time, especially as this country's assets are seized and given to the victorious applicants, most (if not all) countries will halt these egregious practices. Furthermore, would a state that provides torture equipment to another state continue to do so? Once again, I have strong doubts that it would, especially when doing so opens a country up to being sued. The point is that offering a remedy would not only fulfill the legal obligation that already exists under international law but also serve to halt violations from occurring in the first place. States will not continue to violate human rights if there is a strong likelihood that they will be held responsible for doing so.

One other point is that several of the judicial bodies involved in the *Al-Adsani* case based their ruling on the idea that an opposite holding would entail a second burden of refugee protection: the first burden (presumably) is admitting refugees in the first place; the second would be if these refugees were then allowed to proceed against their former state. Yet, what also needs to be pointed out is that in both *Nelson* and *Al-Adsani* the complaining parties were citizens of that state and not refugees.

The second consequence that I want to mention is what the ruling in *Al-Adsani* means for the applicant himself. One of the most disingenuous aspects of the entire opinion is the Court's comment that "there were other, traditional means of redress for wrongs of this kind available to the applicant, namely diplomatic representations or an inter-State claim" (par. 50). One is hard-pressed to understand how the applicant himself could have carried out diplomatic negotiations with a sovereign state (although apparently he claims to have tried). Furthermore, it is simply not possible for an individual to file an inter-state complaint against another state—this, after all, is why it is termed the inter-state complaint system. On the other hand, several international human rights treaties allow individuals to file complaints against states (or at least those states that accede to this). However, it is by no means clear whether a citizen of one state can file an action against a country other than his/her own.

In my view, *Al-Adsani* was indeed a lost opportunity to (finally) get things "right" in the realm of human rights. The whole premise behind international human rights law is that states can no longer hide behind the principle of "state sovereignty." *Al-Adsani* stands for the proposition that countries can continue to use "state sovereignty" as a shield—so long as it is the "sovereignty" of another state that is being protected. What truly seems odd about this entire scenario is that, while the United Kingdom itself can no longer hide behind the principle of "state sovereignty," apparently there is nothing unlawful with allowing another country to do so.

The Domestic Courts of Other State Parties

Many (perhaps all) of the judges involved in *Al-Adsani* were concerned with the potential burden to an "innocent" state if an opposite result had been handed down. That is, one of the recurrent themes was that a country that had absolutely no connection with the human rights violation might be called upon to provide an "effective remedy." An example of this would be if Al-Adsani had brought his complaint against Kuwait in a German court. The point is that Al-Adsani is not a German citizen, and his torture had not taken place in Germany. In fact, Al-Adsani might have no connection whatsoever with the German state. Yet, if the *Al-Adsani* court had reached an opposite conclusion, an "innocent" country like Germany might be held in violation of Article 6 of the ECHR if it rejected a similar kind of claim.

I would imagine that most people (including many of the *Al-Adsani* judges) would be against allowing such a suit to proceed, essentially on the grounds that this case (but also many more like it) would prove to be an incredible burden to the German judiciary (not to mention the overall strain on the German state as well). To help address this, what I propose is a variation whereby states would not be able to invoke sovereign immunity protection—but only as this relates to the domestic courts of countries that are state parties to the same international human rights convention being invoked. Thus, if France and Algeria are both state parties to the Torture Convention (but, say, Angola is not) someone tortured in France should be able to use the domestic courts of Algeria (as well as the domestic courts of any of the other parties to this Convention) in order to sue France for its violation of human rights—but not Angola.

One of the arguments that I have made throughout this book is that international human rights treaties should mean much more than they do. Rather than serving solely as a guideline for how a state should act within its own domestic sphere, the goal of all international human rights treaties is to bring states together to work on some common human rights problem—whether it is torture, discrimination against women, violations of children's rights, and so on. According to my proposal, international human rights treaties should be interpreted in such a way that the courts of one member state will be treated as a state's own (at least with respect to violations of human rights). And if a country cannot invoke sovereign immunity protection at home (and according to international human rights law it is not allowed to protect itself in this fashion) it should not be able to invoke sovereign immunity protection in the courts of any other state party as well.

CONCLUSION

The biggest weakness in all of international human rights law is the lack of enforcement of those rights. Thus, while international human rights law provides for all kinds of rights for individuals, a substantial portion of mankind does not enjoy these rights, and the primary reason for this state of affairs is that there is simply no place, and no means, for enforcing human rights. The fourth step—creating the means by which individuals can enforce their own human rights—is the most important step of all. Toward that end, this chapter sets forth several different proposals. One is to create a permanent International Civil Court where individuals *themselves* could bring a legal action against a state (or states) that have violated these rights. Such a court would seek to complement already existing institutions, most notably, the various regional human rights tribunals as well as the newly created International Criminal Court. A related proposal would be the creation of a World Court of Human Rights. Such a Court would function much like the International Civil Court, only states would be able to limit which human rights violations they could be held accountable for.

There is no question that many states would actively resist the creation of either an International Civil Court or a World Court. What might be more achievable, then, is to employ already existing domestic courts—only the domestic courts in states other than where the human rights violation was carried out. Thus, if a citizen of State A was tortured by agents of State A, this person would be able to bring a suit (against State A) before the courts in some other country. Why should this other state be responsive to this claim? For the simple reason that international human rights law promises victims an "effective remedy."

While this proposal initially might not have an intuitive ring to it, various aspects of this idea have already gained some ground. For one thing, under the *Filartiga* litigation in the United States, individuals who are responsible for directing or carrying out human rights violations in some other land (but who are found and properly served in the United States) have been held to account for their actions.

One thing to note is that these cases—what is commonly referred to as Alien Tort Statute cases—are suits brought against individuals, not against states. Yet, as we have already seen, the entire concept of sovereign immunity has undergone major changes. Many states have adopted the "restrictive" version of sovereign immunity, which means that a state will not be granted immunity for actions of a nonsovereign nature. But there have been other changes as well. One of the most noteworthy involves the 1996 amendments to the Foreign Sovereign Immunity Act whereby governments that "sponsor" terrorism (or at least those states listed by the State Department as "state sponsors of terrorism") can be sued (by U.S. nationals) in American courts.

Unfortunately, vestiges of sovereign immunity protection remain. We examined two cases one by the U.S. Supreme Court (*Saudi Arabia v. Nelson*) and the other by the European Court of Human Rights (*Al-Adsani v. United Kingdom*)—where torture victims sought to hold a state accountable for such actions. However, notwithstanding the fact that the torture victims were nationals of the state where suit was first filed, the ruling court held that there was no violation of either domestic or international law in providing sovereign immunity protection to an offending state. I believe that both *Nelson* and *Al-Adsani* were wrongly decided. In my view, a country that grants sovereign immunity protection to a state that violates human rights—particularly when the violation involves a *jus cogens* norm—has itself committed a human rights violation, albeit of a different magnitude and order.

Both of these cases (especially *Al-Adsani*) can be explained not so much on the basis of the international law itself (which seems fairly clear on this matter) but rather from the fear of the "dire consequences" that would ensue from an opposite holding. Although I believe that the ECHR approached this issue in a narrow-minded fashion—never considering the possibility of class action lawsuits, for example, or the way in which human rights violations would be severely reduced if and when states are (finally) held to account for their actions I do not mean to underestimate the enormous burdens to a state. As a result of this concern for "innocent" states, I provided a variation to this proposal: countries should not be able to invoke the defense of sovereign immunity when they are being sued in the courts of states that are party to the same international human rights treaty. Shared membership in an international human rights treaty means something—or at least it should mean vastly more than it has to date. Countries become a state party to an international human rights treaty because they are concerned with addressing some particular human rights problem—not only within their own territorial borders but also wherever these human rights violations take place. This, after all, is why international human rights law exists in the first place. The point is that member states are not "strangers" to one another, to employ Henry Shue's terminology. Rather, they have bound themselves together to address particular human rights issues, and this will not be achieved—it simply cannot be achieved—by allowing other member states to carry out actions that are in direct contravention of this international treaty.

REFERENCES

Al-Adsani v. United Kingdom. Judgment of November 21, 2001, 34 EHRR 11 (2002).

Alien Tort Statute. 28 U.S.C. Sec. 1350.

Antiterrorism and Effective Death Penalty Act [AEDPA]. 22 U.S.C. Sec. 2377-2378 (2004).

Arrest Warrant of April 11, 2000 (*Democratic Republic of the Congo v. Belgium*) ICJ (2001).

Caplan, Lee. 2003. "State Immunity, Human Rights, and *Jus Cogens:* A Critique of the Normative Hierarchy Theory." *American Journal of International Law* 97:741–81.

Donoho, Douglas. 2006. "Human Rights Enforcement in the Twenty-First Century." *Georgia Journal of International & Comparative Law* 35:1–52.

Donovan, Donald Francis, and Anthea Roberts. 2006. "The Emerging Recognition of Universal Civil Jurisdiction." *American Journal of International Law* 100:142–63.

Filartiga v. Pena-Irala. 630 F. 2d 876 2d Cir. (1980).

Foreign Sovereign Immunity Act [FSIA]. 28 U.S.C. 1602-1611 (2004).

Gibney, Mark. 2002. "On the Need for an International Civil Court." *The Fletcher Forum of World Affairs* 26:47–58.

LaPlante, Lisa. 2004. "Bringing Effective Remedies Home: The Inter-American Human Rights System, Reparations, and the Duty of Prevention." *Netherlands Quarterly of Human Rights* 22/3:347–88.

Mutua, Makau. 1999. "The African Human Rights Court: A Two-Legged Stool?" *Human Rights Quarterly* 21:342–63.

Nowak, Manfred. 2007. "The Need for a World Court of Human Rights." *Human Rights Law Review* 7:251–59.

Regina v. Bow Street Metropolitan Stipendiary Magistrate and Others. Ex parte Pinochet Ugarte (No. 3), judgment of March 24, 1999 Appeal Cases 147 (2000).

Saudi Arabia v. Nelson. 507 U.S. 349 (1993).

Shelton, Dinah. 2005. *Remedies in International Human Rights Law.* 2nd ed. Oxford: Oxford University Press.

Soering v. United Kingdom. App. No. 4038/88 [1989] ECHR 14 (July 7, 1989).

Stephens, Beth, and Michael Ratner. 1996. *International Human Rights Litigation in U.S. Courts.* Ardsley, NY: Transnational Publishers.

Van Schaack, Beth. 2003. "Unfulfilled Promise: The Human Rights Class Action." *University of Chicago Legal Forum* 279:352.

CONCLUSION

This book is about our enormous failure to protect human rights, but it is also about the way in which we could begin to protect the human rights that we proclaim that all people already possess.

The biggest problem is the manner in which states have come to interpret international human rights law. Rather than viewing the myriad of human rights treaties, conventions, and covenants as a means and as an opportunity for undertaking a coordinated and concentrated global effort to address many of the problems that afflict the world, states have made international human rights law into something that is was never intended to be: parochial, timid, ultimately self-serving, and worst of all, terribly ineffective.

What I have attempted to do in these pages is to imagine a much different world, in large part by re-conceptualizing international human rights law itself. In these pages, I have argued that the law on state responsibility should more accurately reflect the extent and the degree to which states help to bring about, or perpetuate, violations of human rights. I have also been very critical of the manner in which states have repeatedly used the notion of territory as a means of avoiding their international human rights obligations altogether—negative and positive obligations alike. And, finally, everyone should have very serious concerns with a system of human rights enforcement that has relied almost exclusively on states policing themselves.

The system that we have created simply has not worked, resulting in what I term a "human rights nightmare." We can, we should, and we must do better than we have.

INDEX

African Commission on Human and Peoples' Rights 119–120

"aid and assistance," in violating human rights 22, 24, 27, 33, 48–49, 55, 57, 123; "war on terror," 38–39. See International Law Commission

Al-Adsani v. United Kingdom (ECHR), 13, 19, 120, 128, 129–138, 141. See also sovereign immunity

Alien Tort Statute (U.S.) 124, 140

Antiterrorism and Effective Death Penalty Act of 1996 (U.S.), 38, 125

Arias, Oscar 38

arms sales, vii–viii, 27

Arms Trade Treaty, 38, 48

Rwanda 54

Bankovic et al. v. Belgium et al. (ECHR), 15, 65–78, 82, 120, 136

Bosnia v. Serbia (ICJ, Genocide Convention case), 31–37

Children's Convention (International Covenant on the Rights of the Child), 4, 102–104

cluster bombs, 50–51

"commercial activities," exception to sovereign immunity, 19, 124–128. See also Foreign Sovereign Immunity Act

Congo v. Belgium (ICJ, Arrest Warrants case), 118

Cyprus v. Turkey (Eur. Comm. H.R.), 74

Darwin's Nightmare, vii, viii, ix, x, 5, 14

Declaration on the Right to Development (U.N.) 108–109

Detainee Treatment Act (U.S.) 80

domestic courts, as means of remedying human rights violations, 18–20, 123–138; state parties to same human rights treaty, 138–139

Draft Articles on State Responsibility, 28–30, 32–37, 48. See also International Law Commission

Economic Covenant (International Covenant on Economic, Social and

Cultural Rights), viii, 3, 16, 44, 90–96; Committee on Economic, Social and Cultural Rights (U.N.), 93–96

"effective remedy," for violations of human rights, 17–19, 116–120, 126–127, 133–134

European Commission on Human Rights, 74

European Convention, 15, 19, 65–78, 129–138. See also jurisdiction

European Court of Human Rights (ECHR), 15, 19, 58, 65–78, 120–121, 129–138

extraordinary rendition, 80–81, 82

extraterritorial application of U.S. (domestic) law, 42

extraterritorial obligations, 2–3, 10, 11, 16–17, 85, 86; inherent in all human rights treaties, 11, 109–111

Flatlow v. Islamic Republic of Iran (U.S.), 39

Food, Special Rapporteur on Right to (Jean Ziegler), 95

Foreign Sovereign Immunity Act (U.S.), 19, 38–39, 124–128, 140

GATT/WTO, 107

Geneva Conventions, 71

Genocide Convention: Bosnia v. Serbia (ICJ), 31–37; Rwanda, 54, 104–105; "influence" standard, to "prevent" genocide, 34–37

Global Gag Order (Mexico City Policy), 51–53

Guantanamo Bay, Cuba, 15–16, 79–80; as refugee processing center, 106. See also "war on terror"

Haitian interdiction program, 15, 58–65

Hamdan v. Rumsfeld (U.S.), 80

human rights: double victimization, 17–18, 117–118 (see also "effective remedy"); failure to recognize responsibilities to people in other states, 1–2, 28; international, lack thereof under international human rights law, 10, 18, 110; legal obligations, 9–10; misunderstanding of, viii, 11; state obligations, extent of, ix, 4–9, 11, 14–16; universality, declarations of, viii, 3–4, 17

Human Rights and Small Arms, U.N. Special Rapporteur (Barbara Frey), 38. See also arms sales

Human Rights Committee (U.N.), 72–73, 96–97, 119, 140

human rights obligations, negative and positive, 5–11, 16, 57, 82, 143

Ilascu and Others v. Moldova and Russia (ECHR), 76

individual complaint system, Optional Protocol for, 72–73, 119

Inter-American Court of Human Rights, 120

International Bill of Rights, viii, x, 3, 88, 90, 96

International Civil Court, proposal for, 18, 120, 121–122

International Court of Justice (ICJ), 14, 18, 21–27, 31–37, 48, 118

International Criminal Court (ICC), 18, 118, 121, 140

International Criminal Tribunal for Rwanda (ICTR), 54, 118

International Criminal Tribunal for Yugoslavia (ICTY), 25–27, 32, 118

International Law Commission, 28–30, 46, 48, 134

International Monetary Fund, 46–47

Inter-state complaint systems, 18, 21, 56, 100, 101, 110, 119, 138
Issa v. Turkey (ECHR), 76–78

Johnson v. Eisentrager (U.S.), 78–80
jus cogens norms, 126, 128–131, 135–136, 141
jurisdiction, within "Europe," 66–78

Lopez v. Uruguay (HRC), 72–73, 97

Maastricht Guidelines on Violations of Economic, Social and Cultural Rights, 44
Military Commissions Act (U.S.), 80
Millennium Declaration (UN), 109
moral obligations, 5–9
Morsink, Johannes, 85, 88

Nicaragua v. U.S. (ICJ), 14, 21–25, 26–27, 30–32
nonrefoulement, principle of, 15, 61–65, 81, 106, 132
Nowak, Manfred, 18, 122–123. See also World Court of Human Rights

Ocalan v. Turkey (ECHR), 74–75

Pinochet, case against, 18, 101, 117, 134, 135
Pogge, Thomas, 4, 9
Political Covenant (International Covenant on Civil and Political Rights), 72–73, 90, 96–98; Human Rights Committee, 72–73, 96–98, 110, 114; "effective remedy," legal obligation to provide, 116–120; Optional Protocol, 72–73, 119 (see also individual complaint system)
primary responsibility of territorial state for protecting human rights,

4 5, 8, 10, 41 46, 103 104, 107–108
Prosecutor v. Tadic (ICTY), 25–28, 32

Rasul v. Bush (U.S.), 78 80
Refugee Act of 1980 (U.S.) 60–61, 64
Refugee Convention, 60–65, 67, 105–107, 132
Rwanda, arms sales to, 53–55, 104–105, 118; French intervention, 54, 105

Sale v. Haitians Centers Council (U.S.), 15, 59–65, "return," meaning of under domestic and international law, 62–65, 82. See also nonrefoulement
Saudi Arabia v. Nelson (U.S.), 19, 124–129, 137, 141. See also Foreign Sovereign Immunity Act
Secondary responsibility for protecting human rights, 41–46, 103–104, 107–108
Shue, Henry, 5 9, 16, 96, 141
Sierra Leone, Special Court, 37
Skogly, Sigrun, 86, 91 92, 94, 98, 102–103
Soering v. United Kingdom (ECHR), 132–133
sovereign immunity, 19, 38, 117–118, 124–138. See also Foreign Sovereign Immunity Act (U.S.); State Immunity Act of 1978 (U.K.)
State Immunity Act of 1978 (UK), 130–131
State Responsibility, control" as wrong standard for state responsibility, 27–28, 31–37; "effective control" standard, 23–27, 32, 35, 39, 48, 74, 77; failure to measure degrees of responsibility, 24, 33, 48–55;

"overall control" standard, 27, 32, 39, 48 (see *Prosecutor v. Tadic*); primary and secondary responsibilities of states, 4–5, 8, 10, 28, 41, 44–45, 48, 94, 103, 107–108; promoting nonresponsibility, 37
state sovereignty, and state responsibility, 1–2, 138

Taylor, Charles, indictment of, 37–38
Torture Convention, 11, 34, 81, 89–102, 117, 119, 126–128, 132; Committee Against Torture (U.N.), 101
Torture, Special Rapporteur on (Manfred Nowak), 122–123. See also, Manfred Nowak, World Court of Human Rights
trade barriers, as source of human rights violations, 49–50

Trail Smelter (U.S. v. Canada), 45–46
Transnational Corporations (TNCs), and violations of human rights, 39–46

Universal Declaration of Human Rights, 2, 85, 88–90
universality of human rights, 2–3, 4, 7, 11
United Kingdom v. Al-Skeini (U.K.), 75–76
United Nations Charter, 28, 86–88, 108

"war on terror," 15, 38, 49, 58, 78–81, 82; Antiterrorism and Effective Death Penalty Act, and state responsibility, 38–39
World Bank, 46–47, 94, 123
World Court of Human Rights, proposal for, 8, 122–123

ABOUT THE AUTHOR

Mark Gibney is the Belk Distinguished Professor at the University of North Carolina at Asheville, where he has taught since 1998. His publications have appeared in such journals as *Human Rights Quarterly, Harvard Human Rights Journal, Fletcher Forum of World Affairs, Boston College International & Comparative Law Journal, Georgetown Immigration Law Journal, Peace Review,* and the *Harvard International Journal of Press/Politics.* Previous books include *Five Uneasy Pieces* (2005) and the edited collection *The Age of Apology: Facing up to the Past* (2007).